I got the Word in me
and I can sing it, you know

I got the Word in me and I can sing it, you know

A Study of the Performed African-American Sermon

Gerald L. Davis

UNIVERSITY OF PENNSYLVANIA PRESS
PHILADELPHIA

Library of Congress Cataloging in Publication Data

Davis, Gerald L.
  I got the word in me and I can sing it, you know.

  Bibliography: p.
  Includes index.
  1. Afro-American preaching. 2. Preaching—
United States. I. Title.
BV4221.D38 1985   251 .008996073   85-2544
ISBN 0-8122-7987-5 (cloth)
ISBN 0-8122-1259-2 (pbk.)

Printed in the United States of America

To
Vera Mae
and
Ephrem, O.C.S.O.

And I want you to know, I got the word in me
And I, I can sing it, you know
I got the word in me, and I don't have to wonder who's with me
I don't care if none of you ain't with me
I don't have to worry about it
'Cause I got the word in my heart
And if I got the word in my heart
He walks with me.

BISHOP ELMER E. CLEVELAND
Ephesians Church of God in Christ, Berkeley

The same beat that Black folks dance to on Saturday night is the same beat that they shout to on Sunday morning. * * * If you hear the beat and do not know what the program is, watch the direction of the shout; if the shout is up and down, it is religious; if it is from side to side, it is probably secular.

REV. DR. WYATT TEE WALKER
Canaan Baptist Church of Christ, New York

Contents

On the "Call" to Preach

I asked Bishop Cleveland if he was "called" to preach. The bishop replied:

> Preachers are born. They are not called, they are born. . . . When you're born, preaching is in you. And when the time comes it stirs, God stirs it up. Bible says, "Stir up the gift that is within you, which are given you from God." So when I begin praying and I really got converted, why then it started up and I began preaching. And I went for a couple of years maybe without acknowledging it. I had to get up to testify and speak and I'd go ahead. I could preach. They said, "Preach!" Oh when they said that, I'd say, "Oh, oh, that isn't the way I want it" and I'd stop. And it just went so bad so long 'til I had to do it, you know. . . . I used to work in a . . . peanut thrashing machine in a tractor and all day I could just hear preaching just like I preach now. I could hear it. Just like somebody put me in a gallery. And I, sometimes I'd look up, see if I could see somebody. . . . And at night, at night I'd go home to bed. I'd go to sleep, I'd go to preaching. I'd wake up in the morning, I'd be tired. Preaching all night. . . . So just when God stir it up, you got to do something about it, and so that's when I gave my heart to God. Why then God stirred up what was in me. So that's the way it is, and I've been knowing it from a boy. And I used to play, me and my sister and other kids would play church, and I'd always be the preacher. And I'd get in the wagon, they'd have boxes and things all around on the ground, and I'd get in the wagon and preach. And I'd feel it just like I do now. Just feel it was taking me over and I'd get where I couldn't stop. I'd get afraid. . . . So a preacher is a preacher, just like I was born Black.

And I asked Bishop Cleveland, "Did you also know how to preach from the time you accepted your gift? . . . Did you know how to preach a good sermon when you first started preaching?" Bishop Cleveland replied: "When I first started preaching, why I could just, I could pick up a sermon from any thought, you know. It's that way now, I guess. I can just, I can get a sermon out of anything."

And I asked Mrs. Smith, a member of Ephesians Church of God in Christ for thirty-two years, to describe Bishop Cleveland as a preacher. Sister Smith responded: "Well, as a preacher, I think they say that you're not born to a thing. But in his category I think he is.

Because anytime of day, anytime of night, that you start talking with him, and especially if you ask him anything concerning the Scripture, then you're going to have a sermon or a message."

ON PREACHING AND STYLE

Ernestine Cleveland Reems, Bishop Cleveland's daughter, is a preacher in her own right and pastors the Center of Hope in East Oakland, California. I asked Pastor Reems to describe her father's preaching. Pastor Reems responded:

> Well, I feel Dad's a preacher, a teacher, a philosopher, you know? . . . Although he didn't finish college, or go to college, he just finished the eighth grade, but to me God has given him great wisdom. And he's a man that reads a lot. He does a lot of reading. And so . . . he has tremendous insight, and he has a sense of reality, and you'll find Dad's preaching is a lot like Jesus. He preaches from parables. And he goes back to his life in the country, on the farm, and he, and he can take such . . . things and, and just, you know, really give you a real understanding as to what God is saying. And I feel like this is the type of preacher he is. He's not a seminary preacher, but he . . . puts it together real well. . . . And he really gets down to a man's level, and preaches a gospel . . . that you can understand. It's good news. And that's what the gospel is. I like eloquent speakers, and Shakespeare, and all of that. Dad doesn't bring all that in. But man, he has straight wisdom. And philosophy. It's just fantastic.

I asked Pastor Reems if there were significant differences between her preaching and her father's preaching. Pastor Reems replied:

> Not really. I just feel that . . . I'm . . . aware of the times. And I've really tried to preach messages that are relevant to . . . what's happening today. . . . I think Dad has a lot more experience than I have. A lot more knowledge than I have. And there's just no way that I could preach like he preach, because he preaches from actual experience. He's eighty [laughs] years old, and he knows a lot more than I do. . . . But I really try to deal with what's happening today. And I feel that's the way you can really reach people. . . . And I try to gear my messages to, to what's happening today, and what's what, you know, how we should really remember the times in which we are living. I preach a lot about the Middle East; all of that relates. Everything that's happening today the Bible saw already, you know, foresaw it, and really speaks of it. So there is where I try to gear messages to reach young people. And if you get down to what they're talking about, and what's happening with them, you can reach them. So, I think . . . I preach a lot like Dad, because I

do a lot of teaching. . . . And then if I think I'm losing the audience, I'll excite them and get 'em a little happy, so that I can get their attention again. And I think this is what speakers should really be aware of. You shouldn't be just up there, just talking. You should hold your audience and keep their attention, and get to your point.

And I asked Mrs. Smith, a long-time member of Bishop Cleveland's congregation to describe the bishop's special gifts as a preacher. Sister Smith responded: "Well, to me, if I understand that correctly, he has a lovely deliverance, and he is the type that speak a lot of parables, and he'll keep you laughing and yet he say, 'I'm not telling this for you to laugh,' but when he gets through with a parable, you're able to see the thing that he's trying to present to you."

Following a church service, I queried Mr. Dixon, a member of Bishop Cleveland's congregation for twenty-five years, on Bishop Cleveland's preaching style. I asked Mr. Dixon how he felt service went that day. He replied: "Well, service was just glorious today. We had a wonderful time in the Lord."

I asked Mr. Dixon what, in his estimation, made Bishop Cleveland a great preacher? Mr. Dixon answered: "Well, that's a good question. My estimation is that it's his dedication to God. I think that's what makes him a great preacher."

I pursued the question. Does Bishop Cleveland's preaching style have a particular appeal to you? Mr. Dixon replied: "Very much so. Yes, very much so."

I asked Mr. Dixon to describe Bishop Cleveland's style. Mr. Dixon responded:

> I said his dedication to God, and that's what it takes to be better for God, is the fact that you're dedicated. It's just like being dedicated to your profession as a photographer or a cameraman or whatever your position is, the more dedicated you are to it the better you becomes. And God is able to make you better, and that is the fact that I hold to that has made him better is his dedication to God. . . . I believe the thing that makes him so great is in his parables that he uses, that he's preached the same in regards to parables as he did, say, fifty years ago, and today he's using the same simple parables that the ordinary person would be able to comprehend his preaching. And I think that helps to make him a great preacher.

I asked Mr. Dixon if Bishop Cleveland quoted more frequently from the Bible now than he did in his earlier years. Mr. Dixon replied: "Well . . . I think so, because the Word is the thing. . . . The Word is quick and it's sharp and it's powerful. And then the fact that he uses this is a help and that definitely makes his ministry more powerful."

"Is it a source of pride for you that Bishop Cleveland knows the Bible so well?" I asked. "Well . . . yes, I would take pride in the fact that he's been my pastor for twenty-five years, and I've been on his ministry for that length of time, so naturally I take some pride in it."

Preface

Paul Carter Harrison writes:

> The preacher is a spiritualist who, quite like the traditional medicine
> man, mediates between spirit and corpus, light and shadow, manipulat-
> ing all the forces in mode with proper wordforce (Nommo) so that the
> spirit will be revealed. . . . The preacher, having been assigned the task
> of orchestrating all aspects of the mode into harmonious relationships
> uses a script, a story-book—the Bible—as the object source of his
> storytelling to bridge myth with reality; the spirit must come through
> strongly . . . if the social and moral directives of the story are to be
> accepted by the congregation/community. As any good stage director,
> the preacher must utilize the proper devices—phonically, physically,
> and visually—to produce images that will urge the emotions of the com-
> munity to coalesce around the goals of the ceremony: once the entire
> mode has become unified, the total experience becomes a testament of
> the truth—and the truth don't move!—a revelation of reality.[1]

Parting with a convention established by those African-American
colleagues whose writings on aspects of the Black church have preceded mine, I will not claim a consistent participatory background in
the affective institution known as "the Black church." This is not to admit that I am "unchurched" in the Black community context, however.
While a young Protestant student in a Catholic school—Church of the
Resurrection School on 151st Street between McCombs Place and Sev-
enth Avenue in Harlem—I was required to go to religious instruction
once a week. I recall a particular fondness for entering the darkened
church sanctuary and lighting the votive candles. I would dutifully
genuflect and say a prayer, but it was quite some time before I was
to appreciate that one left appropriate monetary contributions following the lighting of a votive candle in the Catholic church. The ritual
and dark majesty of it all attracted me, a curious addiction I retain to
this day.

For Protestant Sunday school, I went to Saint Marks African
Methodist Episcopal (A.M.E.) Church on Convent Avenue in Harlem.
Saint Marks was more Episcopal in spirit than it was either African or
Methodist. The Reverend Dr. Sweeney was a learned man and dis-

coursed rather than preached. I recall that he was kindly and rather elegant, "fair-skinned" with "straight" hair, wore wire-rimmed glasses, and was slightly corpulent—he was perfect for the comfortable congregation. Never, never did I hear an untoward utterance from the congregation during church service, save for a discreet cough and a polite raising of voices during congregational hymn singing.

My sister and I would walk home some Sundays and frequently stop outside of fundamentalist, charismatic churches to mimic the active praising and testifying we could hear from inside. It "made sense" to me somehow.

Mother Caldwell, who took care of us after school while my parents were at work, was an Israelite, a Black Jew. Sometimes she would take us to her temple on 125th Street near Eighth Avenue for services. I do not remember much of those times, just the images of women in white and men in black and the sense that I was, somehow, party to something powerful if furtive.

Frequently, I would go to the Baptist church pastored by a friend's father and listen to the Reverend Mr. Matthews preach and watch the congregation "witness." It all seemed so mystical, so magical, sometimes wondrous, always gripping from my vantage point in the rear pews. Imprinting of a sort, I guess. But no matter, the power of the African-American performed Word has stayed with me. Certainly no one event is more compelling for me than the performance of the Word—God's codebook for secular living and sacred example—and the masterful, electric interpretation of that codebook, through the use of expressive language systems by the accomplished African-American preacher.

The preacher's community personae are as varied as the verbal systems he employs in his pulpit performance. Historically, he has been shaman, priest, poet, politician, definer and keeper of ritual, chief, and sometimes traitor, but always the sanctioned guardian of the Word, that peculiar repository of knowledge and wisdom, cultural sanctity and cognition, personal and group worth. And he has been and continues to be the butt of innumerable jokes which turn on his supposed gluttony, lust, avarice, and ironically, his malapropisms. Yet he and his craft are so pivotal in the workings of African-American cultural forms that if one is to understand the structural complexities of language invention and expressive language forms in African America, it is to the work of the sermon craftsman in performance that one must turn.

When I began this work on the performed African-American sermon many years ago, I intended it to change forever the way folklorists and social scientists looked at an expressive form (and its

African-American performers) that was a commonplace in my life but about which I actually knew very little. That is, I intuitively knew something about the sermon as it was performed in Black churches, but I had not considered it intellectually. This study is more humbly offered now. I have been humbled by the impatience and forbearing of African-American preachers and their congregation members and supporters as I have continued to gather "massive amounts of data," and I have been sobered by the incisive materials on the subject published in recent years by colleagues who share a sense of advocacy as strong as my own.

In this study I want to answer a query only an academic would probably raise: How does one know when a performed African-American sermon is "good"? This is not to say that African-American congregations are not concerned with "good" sermon-making or "good" preaching. They most certainly are. The test for the success is not so much how convincing I have been in arguing my case before my fellow academic colleagues but how closely I have been able to approximate, in scholarly language, the same process Black folk employ in evaluating a "successful" sermon.

Given the wide currency of aspects of the sermon event or sermon style in African-American public address contexts, secular as well as sacred, an answer to the query posed above becomes a matter of interest for those concerned with aesthetics and ethnoaesthetics, poetics, sociolinguistics, folklore, and a host of related disciplines and sub-disciplines that focus on language usage in culture and society. The sub-rosa agenda is the articulation of an African-American sermon. Does such a thing exist? I think it does, and I hope *I Got the Word in Me and I Can Sing It, You Know* makes that case.

Several people have been helpful in bringing me to this point in my research perspectives. While I was a graduate student at the University of Pennsylvania, Dan Ben-Amos, mentor and very good friend, was relentless in his insistence on excellence and clarity. For a number of years John Szwed provided balance, strong support, and ways of looking at African-American materials that are dynamic and original. Kenneth Goldstein and his wife, Rochelle, were good listeners during difficult personal moments in my graduate years. And Alan Dundes suggested the sermon as a fruitful area of inquiry many years ago during a well-remembered walk along Dwight Way in Berkeley. Indeed, it was Dundes who strongly encouraged me to continue my graduate study for the doctorate in folklore. And in personal correspondence and through his writings, Roger Abrahams continues to fire my mind and academic spirit in ways few others have been able to do. Perhaps someday I will apologize to him for my murderous thoughts following my first reading of *Deep Down in the Jungle*.

In the years since Phil Peek and I were graduate students together at Berkeley, he has patiently listened to my various babblings and commented sagely when some of the babblings began to take shape as more fully formed research ideas and concepts. He and Pat continue to be good and strong friends. I met James Fernandez at a party Rutgers University anthropologists gave for their Princeton University colleagues at the New Brunswick home of the late and sorely missed Vera Green. For years I had admired Fernandez's research and was delighted when he asked to read a copy of this manuscript in an earlier form. His subsequent comments were both useful and encouraging. In ways far too numerous to catalog here, Wesley Huss encouraged me to be trusting of my perceptions and intuitions, always.

It is more difficult to thank those of my African-American colleagues who have been "family" over the years. Ernest Dunn, Gladys-Marie Fry, the late Vera Green, Stephen Henderson, Walton Johnson, Steven Jones, Johnnie Lacey, Cliff Lashley, Isaac Moore, Kathryn Morgan, Erskine Peters, Adrienne Seward, Marilyn White, and William Wiggins have provided countless opportunities for discussion and argument on my approaches to this material and to the study of African-American culture more generally. Ollie Bryant, with whom I spent long and loving hours, and her two sons, Frank III and David, were generous with their time, their hospitality, and their love. These friends provided an emotional security and uncompromising criticism as I struggled to know more of the nuances and power of the African-American preacher's art and craft.

An especially profitable discussion of some of the ideas in this present work occurred at Drew Theological Seminary during an afternoon of conversation with the seminary's Black caucus. It was the first time I had been able to share my work with African-American theologians, and I am deeply appreciative of the sharp, insightful discussion and the expressions of strong interest in the work. And especially I am grateful for Dean Trulear's hand in arranging the Drew meeting.

Tom Slaughter, a Black philosopher and former Rutgers University colleague, brought my consideration of aesthetics and African-American performance in the context of African-American preaching to the attention of Howard McGary. McGary, as president of the New York Society for the Study of Black Philosophy, extended an invitation to me to share my thoughts with the society on a blustery afternoon in April 1984 in the Manhattan apartment of Al Prettyman. The comments following my remarks were enormously helpful in clarifying my thoughts in this area, and I am indebted to Slaughter and McGary and members of that august association for their difficult and challenging queries and their strong support for my work.

Very special thanks go to the ministers and congregations whose names and lives are so central to the representation in these pages. I am particularly grateful for the trust of Bishop E. E. Cleveland, Sister Grace Smith, and Mr. and Mrs. Dixon of Ephesians Church of God in Christ in Berkeley, California. Ephesians Chairman of the Board Elder Hervy Luster and Mrs. Luster, with great love and patience, "kept me straight and honest" during my workings with Bishop Cleveland, Pastor Reems, and the congregations of Ephesians and the Center of Hope.

I would be remiss if I did not acknowledge my new and unrestrained respect for the skill and craft of the various editors at the University of Pennsylvania Press who contributed to the shaping of the final form of this work. John McGuigan, who is no longer with the Press, made insightful and valuable suggestions for revisions when an earlier version of this manuscript was submitted for publication consideration. Kathleen Robinson and Margaret Connelly were attentive and caring in their shepherding of this work and this author through the early twists and turns of the publishing labyrinth. Ingalill Hjelm has been tough but always available, helpful, and supportive. And Joanne Ainsworth's skill as copy editor is nothing short of awesome.

I am especially grateful for the support of the Rutgers University Research Council for a subvention of publication grant. And I am deeply appreciative of the advice and guidance of Dr. Tilden Edelstein, Dean of Rutgers' Faculty of Arts and Sciences, and Dr. C. F. Main of the Rutgers Office of Research and Sponsored Programs.

Finally, a special acknowledgment goes to my father and mother, Lewis and Doris Davis, who have been patient and wonderfully supportive and "who made all of this possible," to my sisters Melba and Janice, and to my brother Brian, and to my son Craig who continued to love this bear even when he roared.

Introduction

The three preachers whose sermons are used in this study were selected as much for their dissimilarities in personality and presentation
as for their proximity to the traditions of African-American preaching.
His Grace, King Louis H. Narciss, D.D., founded the Mount Zion
Spiritual Temple, Inc., over forty years ago. From his international
headquarters in Oakland, King Narciss presides over an association of
temples and congregations in Detroit, Sacramento and Richmond in
California, Houston, Orlando, New York City, and Washington, D.C.[1]
Deeply impressed by the organization of the British monarchy, His
Grace is attended by a retinue of princesses, princes, ladies (in-waiting),
and Queen Mothers. Periodically he anoints others into the privi-
leged circle in a ceremony resembling "knighting" rituals. The Rever-
end Dr. Carl J. Anderson, pastor of Saint John's Missionary Baptist
Church in Oakland, is well-thought of and well-regarded in the Bay
Area (San Francisco-Berkeley-Oakland) as a "good" preacher. Reverend
Anderson heads a fairly large and moderately progressive congregation.
In many ways, he is the prototypical contemporary urban African-
American preacher blending the sophistication and savvy of the successful urban politician and businessman with the earthiness and
mother wit of the Black Southern rural church tradition. Bishop E. E.
Cleveland, whose sermons are the focus of this study, is the least self-
conscious, most traditional, and most accessible of the three preachers. Cleveland's "You're Just Not Ready" was selected as the key sermon
for this study because the sermon illustrates characteristics and other
considerations found commonly in the sermons of African-American
preachers and in other modes of African-American oral expression. Im-
plicit in this statement are factors of aesthetics, history, ethnophi-
losophy, and cosmology, all of which bear heavily on the preacher's
interpretation of events, and the generation of certain and very specific narrative structures.

Some men seem to own the spaces through which they walk. Not
from the arrogance of newly bestowed and unaccustomed power or the
inflation of ego which can result from unwary acquiescence to vanity
but from the simple majesty of spirit and soul—and perhaps from the
mantle of quiet and certain authority borne as a burden of birthright

and as a gift which settles, even after eighty years, uneasily on the shoulders. Elmer E. Cleveland, pastor of Ephesians Church of God in Christ in Berkeley and Los Angeles, and bishop of the Northern California Jurisdiction of the Church of God in Christ, struck me that way at our first meeting.

Bishop Cleveland is the most fundamentalist of the three preachers whose sermons figure prominently in this study. Cleveland combines the conventional theologies of the African-American Methodist and Baptist churches in a broadly affecting, expressive preaching style. Because of his heavy use of parables and Scripture and images no longer part of the current worldview of many younger members of his congregation, Cleveland is sometimes called an "old-fashioned" preacher, which carries the suggestion that he is no longer in touch with contemporary events.[2] Unlike many of his non–African-American fundamentalist (or charismatic) colleagues, Cleveland does not accept the inerrancy of the Bible in matters of faith, historical accuracy, or prophecy. The Bible, for Cleveland, is a record of codified experiences, a guide drawn selectively from the lives and considerations of those who have participated in exemplary humanistic achievement. Cleveland is not concerned with arguments challenging the authenticity of the events depicted in the Bible. For him, the Bible is a statement on the ideal form and quality of the Christian life and must be broadly interpreted for the present-day lives of his congregations and audiences. It is in this sense that Cleveland is a fundamentalist preacher.

But more than content, fundamentalism, for Cleveland, is also a matter of style. Certainly Bishop Cleveland knows the essential doctrines of fundamentalism: the virgin birth of Christ; the physical resurrection of Christ; the inerrancy of the Bible in every detail; the imminent, physical second coming of Christ.[3] But rarely will his sermons derive from or even include these themes. Instead, Cleveland's themes and sermon illustrations are directed toward "ethical purity and moral perfection of character," and any image culled from the Bible for use in a sermon must hold opportunity for the uniting of the sacred with the profane.[4] Or at least there must be ample latitude, in the image, for the sacred example to be made obvious through profane illustration. For Cleveland, sermon themes are Janus icons. Consider, for example, the following profane illustrations/sacred example set taken from Cleveland's sermon of February 11, 1981 (this sermon, by the way, was of an extraordinary, almost epic, length):

> 1021   Whole lot of folks, they, ju . . . getting to church, say they got
> religion

And they, they done quit drinking
Whiskey and beer and stuff
They say, "Well, I don't get drunk like I used to
1025 Before I got religion"
Say, "Course if I want to drink some
I'll go buy me some good stuff and go to bed and be decent"
So you ain't rested, you just drinking in bed
Some say, "I used to curse near about every other word I said
1030 Curse at the drop of a hat
Drop it myself
But since I've got religion
I don't curse that-a-way now
But I curse if you make me mad
1035 Make me mad
Make me mad and I'll curse"
Get up and say I'm a liar
You ain't rested
You just rationalizing on your cursing
1040 Course shacking, man, got to be a big thing going now
But years ago it wasn't so
But there always been some shackers
You know, some said, "You know,
Before I got religion, that man, why I lived with him
1045 We lived together
But was . . . since I got religion
We've never lived together a night since
[Pause]
Course he come to see me sometime"
[Congregational laughter and applause]
So you ain't
1050 You ain't resting
HOW YOU GOING TO REST IF YOU'RE GETTING THE WORD OF GOD?
LET THE WICKED FORSAKE HIS WAY
Unrighteous his thoughts
Let him turn unto the Lord
1055 And the Lord will have mercy on him
[unclear]
Didn't He say so?
What is the grace of God?
The grace of God [unclear]
1060 The grace of God that save you from your sins
Amazing Grace

How sweet the sound
That saved a wretch like me
The grace of God
1065   That greatest salvation
Have appeared unto all men
Teaching us and
Denying ungodliness
And worldly lust
1070   And we shall live soberly, righteously, and Godly
In this present world
1072   Sheeew!

The typed phrasing of the sermons in the texts of this study represents the lines as they were spoken by the preachers. No attempt was made to impose a metrical sensibility on the phrasings or phrases. Shorter lines were delivered with a staccato phrasing broken usually by slight pauses to indicate the completion of a phrase. Larger ideas were usually marked by verbal style modification, termination of the staccato style or resumption of a measured, even-toned prose style.

Cleveland and African-American preachers generally can be considered "fundamentalists" because of the manner in which they structure sermons in performance. The set used as the illustration above is a fundamental or basic unit of sermon organization. And most African-American performed sermons are composed of these units cast in a serial structure. These units, quite simply, provide for the balance of concrete secular or profane example against generalized sacred principles, with the weight of the unit, as a narrative form, being carried by the secular or profane hemiunit. This is apparently an almost historical sacred narrative organizational structure among African-Americans, and it may have an African provenance. But both the use of the fundamental unit as the foundation of the African-American performed sermon structure and a sort of quasi-ethnical fundamentalism in the organization of content, which may include glossolalic speech as a performance mode, characterize Cleveland's prototypic sermon performance style and may account for his reputation as an "old-fashioned" preacher.

On Perspective and Method

In their considerations of emic analysis, Kenneth Pike and Alan Dundes chart the general direction of this study of the narrative functions of the constituent elements of the performed African-American sermon. Pike writes, "An emic approach must deal with particular events as parts of larger wholes to which they are related and from which they obtain their ultimate significance. A unit must be studied, not in isolation, but as part of a total functioning componential system within a total culture." In his subsequent examination of emic analysis in the structural study of folklore, which includes an illuminating discussion of Pike's conceptualization of etic and emic approaches to analysis, Dundes writes that the nature of the emic approach is "mono-contextual [and] structural."[5]

Because Dundes, after Pike, observes that emic units are "empirically observable structural [units] . . . which may be discovered through the application of quasi-linguistic techniques," it is useful also to have in mind Dundes's thinking on the nature of units. Dundes writes,

> Units are utilitarian logical constructs of measure which, though admittedly relativistic and arbitrary, permit greater facility in the examination and comparison of the materials studied in the natural and social sciences. It is important that units be standards of one kind of quantity (e.g., units of heat, length, and so forth). Units can be conceived as being abstractions of distinct entities which may be combined to form larger units or broken down into smaller units. There is an infinitude of units since they are man-made categorical attempts to describe the nature of objective reality. . . . A minimal unit may thus be defined as the smallest unit useful for a given analysis.[6]

Dundes also notes that the terms "etic" and "emic" were "coined by using the last portions of the words phonetic and phonemic."[7]

At the heart of the emic approach to culture-specific narrative analysis is a consideration which is consistent with the intent of this examination of the African-American sermon and its various elements. If an emic approach is employed in the analysis of an ethnic narrative structure, then a commitment is in fact being made to "discover" those generating ideas, or creating philosophies, that are culturally based, that support the narrative structure in performance, and that provide for the evaluation of the narrative structure by culture members. If the African-American sermon and the units of which it is composed are to be understood in the context of African-American culture, the units of the sermon as they are employed in performance must be regarded as the products of a conscious, rationalizing sensibility. That sensibility is manifested as principles of sermon performance, or more grandly, structural creating philosophies. The task of this study, therefore, is to describe the character and function of the constituent elements of the African-American sermon and to articulate the series of rationalizing

ideas that result in a particular narrative element occupying a specialized place in the structure of that sermon.

Three important premises which helped to define significant areas
of the approach to the study, and which underpin the study's emic
framework, need to be identified. Each is deserving of a study focus in
its own right, but that prominence is inappropriate in the restricted
focus of the present study.

The first premise concerns the ahistorical character of the sermon
analysis. Beyond an initial statement that African-American preached
sermons share a common geohistorical source, no attempt has been
made to identify the historical developments used to distinguish one
African-American church group from another. The difficulties in such
an enterprise would be considerable. A 1977 study which included a
section on African-American church bodies by "denominational affiliation" listed fifty-three such bodies loosely affiliated within Black Methodist, Holiness, Trinitarian Pentecostal, Baptist, Primitive Baptist, New
Thought, Psychic, Jewish (Hebrew), and Islamic confederations. And
this listing did not include such groups as Catholics, Episcopalians, and
Congregationalists, which are not "historically" Black but which have
formed all African-American congregations. Indeed, as recently as July
1982, there was a major split in the Church of God in Christ organization, resulting in the establishment of yet another significant Black
church body, the United Church of God in Christ. Each of the church
bodies has its own sense and description of its historical development,
only minimally incorporating the history of the larger denomination
with which it may have some affiliation.[8]

To be sure, there are quasi-theological differences between the
various African-American denominations and church bodies. But these
differences are not, by and large, manifest in the narrative structures
of the preached African-American sermon. In terms of its structural
characteristics, a sermon preached by Bishop Cleveland of the Ephesians Church of God in Christ will be virtually identical to a sermon preached by the Reverend Dr. Anderson, a Missionary Baptist
preacher. The sermon structure identified in this study as African-
American describes sermons preached from hundreds of Black pulpits
across America, without regard to denominational affiliation. That sermon structure is cultural.

The second premise focuses on the geographic range of the sermon
model generated as a result of this research. How widely dispersed is
the sermon model considered in this study to be African-American?
The core materials for the study were collected in northern California.
African-American friends and acquaintances who listened to early for-

mulations of this material were asked to evaluate what they heard in terms of their own backgrounds and experiences in urban and rural southern, eastern, and midwestern American communities. As a result of these responses and in order to test study hypotheses and conclusions in the field, supplementary sermon performances were studied from other areas around the country. During the six years between the collection of the core corpus and the preparation of the initial study results, the hypotheses were further evaluated against commercially produced field recordings of sermon performances and sermons preached at church services I attended. The correlation between the product of the analyses—the generated sermon prototype or model— and actual performed sermons was high. Subsequent lectures on my analyses of sermons and coordinated visits to African-American churches by my classes, and recognition of the structures of the sermons by my classes, confirmed that my findings described the sermon faithfully. That is, there seemed to be a performed sermon structure that could be found in most African-American communities.

The third premise had to do with the impact of mass communications media on the performed African-American sermon. Although some of the original corpus of sermons were taken from radio broadcasts, and a significant portion of the supporting materials were taken from commercial recordings, the structures, forms, and aesthetic dimensions of the sermon were not noticeably influenced by the superimposition of media demands. Even the length of a broadcast service was frequently not bent to the needs of broadcast programming. Services were picked up in progress. If the allotted air time ended before the preacher's sermon or before the major prayer, the service was simply faded under the station announcer's voice. The announcer would provide the name and location of the church, the name of the church's pastor, and the sponsor before going to station identification.

An aspect of the third premise gained increasing importance as the study expanded: a concern to know more of the psychological and social properties of sound production deployed by the preacher in sermon performance. Tapes fed through a sound analyzer designed by Daniel Goode, an electronic music composer and a former member of the Livingston College (Rutgers University) music department, indicated that articulated sound, as distinguished from articulated words, carries semantic affect in the context of African-American narrative performance. Frequently such sounds would be responded to by a congregation as if, or in the same manner as if, the sounds were words. Two of the three preachers whose sermons are used in this study conduct the most affective, emotive part of their sermons in sound bands considerably beyond the narrow range most commonly used in pulpit preaching. Potentially this area was one of the more exciting components of the study, although admittedly the most speculative.

THE DATA AND SOME CONTEXTUAL CONSIDERATIONS

The principal body of sermons for the study was collected in Oakland and Berkeley, California, from April to June 1969. To support the California corpus, I studied a supplementary set of sermons from Nashville, Detroit, Chicago, Philadelphia, and Tampa.

Several of the sermons in the California corpus were taped from church services broadcast over radio stations covering the San Francisco–Oakland–Berkeley listening area.[9] These materials were useful in analyses of texts and components of the African-American sermon and in generating a working model of the structure of the African-American sermon. But because the recording equipment was of marginal quality, certain valuable high and low frequencies were distorted beyond recovery in a subsequent attempt to analyze the characteristics of sound by feeding the tapes through sound analyzers. This material would have added substantially to the data derived from analyses of the properties and functions of sound which must accompany other analyses of the performed sermon if it is to be fully understood.

Commercial field recordings were used for part of the supplementary corpus. I collected other sermons in the supplementary corpus while attending church services in Philadelphia during the fall and winter of 1969, in Tampa in 1970 and 1971, and during two field trips to Charleston and Johns Island, South Carolina, in January and May 1971.[10] This was a valuable body of material and supported the finding that the African-American sermon model developed from the California corpus was replicable in African-American pulpits nationally. Although national distribution of the model developed here is not a central point of the study, it is useful to note that as groups migrate they carry with them those units of culture and society that are perceived as integral to the maintenance of the unique character of the group.

Many of the members of the congregations I visited considered the affective preaching style of their pastors to be "southern." Respondents made a distinction between preachers, who "preached from the Spirit" or who were seemingly spontaneous and unrehearsed in their performance of sermons, and ministers, who addressed congregations from prepared texts and with muted emotion. Some respondents stated a misconception found commonly within and without African-American communities: ministers who used prepared texts were usually university or seminary trained. Since my inquiries were directed toward eliciting attitudes and assessments of affective sermon performance, it became clear that, in the thoughts of respondents, "university training" compromised the desirable oral performance abilities of some preachers, even though well-educated preachers are highly prized as pastors. In any event, the ability to respond to, engage, and raise spiritual energies during the performance of a sermon is considered to be an indispensable part of the preacher's art and skill. The minister who does not "raise the Spirit" through the artful manipulation of "the Word" is no less a man of God, however. He is simply not a good preacher or master of African-American pulpit style. His pulpit style is not of the "South."[11]

The U.S. South is a complex, little understood phenomenon in the worldview of African-American people.[12] At the most fundamental, sensate levels, the South is regarded as "roots," a vaguely perceived but powerful point of reference that secures personality clusters in this geographic region. In a cosmologic sense this concept of "roots" also unites African-Americans with a network that has both historical and contemporary significance. Many African-Americans who migrated from the South as long ago as thirty years, as recently as thirty days, regard the region as "backward" and "country," although the South is in many ways more progressive than other areas of the nation. Paradoxically, these same persons and many thousand others return annually to the region for high school reunions, church homecomings, family reunions, funerals, and vacations. The South is a secure place of renewal, of contact with humanizing spirits, of communication with the souls of Black folk.[13]

In recent years, African-American social intellectuals and political activists have come to view the South as the region in which a new and vigorous power and wealth is emerging for African-Americans. Disillusioned and frustrated neorevolutionaries of the 1960s now pragmatically and soberly view the U.S. South as the region in which progressive experiments in social and economic programming can be attempted. Recently published slave testimonies belie the popular fiction of the area. We now know that slaves frequently kept plantations afloat by loaning money to plantation owners; that "cracker" and "nigger" frequently lived as co-equals; that some plantations were Black owned and managed; that even many of the courtly ways popularly known as "southern tradition" may have been "borrowed" from Africans by plantation societies.[14] These ideas bear out the substance of respondents' identification of the affective pulpit style of the African-

American preacher as "southern." It is a unique style. It is a style de-
rivative of an African ethos.

Not all scholars share a common view on the matter of the origins
of African-American preaching style, however. John Blassingame, Don
Yoder, and Bruce Rosenberg find that the style identified as "southern"
is neither African nor African-American.[15] They contend that the style
developed from slaves' mimicking of white Baptist and Calvinist itinerant preachers who moved from plantation to plantation during the
years of slavery in the United States. They are in agreement with
E. Franklin Frazier on this point. There was a time in his research
when Frazier was committed to a perspective that demanded recognition of the "fact" that "from the beginning . . . because of the manner
in which Negroes were captured in Africa and enslaved, they were
practically stripped of their social heritage."[16] Frazier's pronouncement
was consistent with his determination that African slaves were almost
totally denuded of distinct African-based cultural behaviors in the
American context. Unwittingly, Frazier became a principal proponent
of the "invention of the Negro" school, a position he later modified.

In the absence of firm grounding in African materials, scholars might be excused for concluding that affective African-American
preaching has European, rather than African, antecedents. But the literature is now sufficiently extensive on this point to warrant a reassess-
ment of the European antecedent contention. Blassingame, Yoder, and
Rosenberg could have safely observed that the sermon style, if not
theology, they hold to be European has historic precedent in the affective religious and secular narrative systems of several West, Central,
East, and southern African groups.[17]

A more compelling and engaging aspect of this discussion of origins for affective preaching style is provided by Walton Johnson in his
research on the history of the African Methodist Episcopal (A.M.E.)
church in southern Africa.[18] Johnson notes that African-American affective preaching, derived from both secular and sacred African narrative
systems, was likely reintroduced into southern Africa by African-
American missionaries, who have been active in the area since the late
eighteenth century. Johnson's thesis compares favorably with the literature on the return of African slaves to Liberia and Sierra Leone from
the New World. Several social historians have noted that as slaves,
both freed and escaped, migrated from various West Indies ports to lo-
cations on the east coast of the United States and Canada (and from
there to Africa), they carried with them units of non-African cultural
systems. In light of this information, the maintenance of the European
antecedent theory seems archaic.

The African-American sermon and the sermon environment are rich and complex events. A complete analysis of the African-American sermon in performance must capture visual elements, trace foot patterns and arm gestures, as well as record the words and analyze the structures of the genre. A considerable part of the interaction that goes on between a preacher and his congregation is visual. Oftentimes the decision to truncate a line or extend a phrase is made in response to a visual or vocal cue provided by a respected member of the congregation.

During my 1971 field trip to Johns Island, South Carolina, I attempted to film an African-American preacher and his congregation. The attempt was relatively unsuccessful. Without a baffle or an electric motor, my sixteen millimeter camera was too noisy and intrusive and broke the congregation's concentration on the preacher and his sermon. When the preacher finally glowered at me, I put the camera away.

Ten years later, in 1981, I was able to produce *The Performed Word*, a one-hour ethnodocumentary which argues that the Black church is fundamental to understanding African-American performance, particularly language-based performance.[19] The completed film, the first in a projected series of three related film projects, contains only a minimal amount of footage focused on the complex of visual interactions between preacher and congregation. At a future date, footage unused in *The Performed Word* will be assembled, principally for classroom and research use, so that we can analyze in greater detail a variety of visual folkloristic issues.

In an earlier version of this manuscript, I suggested that this study of the structure of the African-American sermon might benefit structural and paralinguistic studies of other forms of narrative and nonnarrative expressive African-American performance. In particular, I had a structural study of the blues in mind. However, the Rev. Jesse Jackson's important 1984 presidential campaign (which might have been less successful had Rep. Shirley Chisolm not "tested the waters" some years earlier) raises anew interest in ancillary structural studies of African-American performance forms, especially in the import and impact of African-American sermonry on national politics and speechmaking.

African-American sermon performance in national political contexts is certainly not a new phenomenon. The Reverend Dr. Martin Luther King, Jr., and many of his associates, including Jackson, were African-American preachers. And King's memorable "I Have A Dream" sermon preached from the steps of the Lincoln Memorial in Washington, D.C., during the historic March on Washington in 1963 was the quintessential adaptation of the performed African-American sermon structure to national and international political purpose. Although King was certainly a towering national and international personality, in the popular mind, he was fundamentally an African-American preacher. Indeed, King did not seek any other primary definition.

What is so fascinating about Jackson's presidential candidacy is that in a few short months a shift could be observed in Jackson's style, substance, and syntax, from African-American preacher-cum-American politician to American politician utilizing the expressive characteristics of Black sermon performance in the accomplishment of his goals and mission. In the early stages of his candidacy, Jackson's attempts to accommodate sermon structure to the particular demands of political content in his public speechmaking were almost comical. His metaphors were skewed. His timing was off. His attempts to articulate his hallmark rhyming couplets fell flat. Nothing seemed to come together for him. But finally he found the formula and from that point on he could be electrifying as an orator on the platform, at the lectern, or in the pulpit. Nowhere is this transition more clearly marked, and in evidence, than in Jackson's historical keynote July 17th address to the 1984 National Democratic Convention. Apparently deciding that he was a national candidate for the American presidency, Jackson assumed all of the trappings of that august image and began fumbling his way, ineptly, through his prepared speech. But part of the genius of the African-American performed sermon structure is that, in the hands of a talented preacher, it permits and allows for instant adjustment. Apparently realizing that his adopted American political speechmaking style was not achieving his desired ends, Jackson transformed his oratorical mode, as he was speaking, to the performed sermon structure this study analyzes. The rest, as the saying goes, was history. Jackson regained confidence as he reclaimed his preaching métier. His moral sense of outrage found a glorious articulation base in the African-American sermon structure that it could not find in the more restrictive American speechmaking style. Hardened delegates—all hues of his "Rainbow Coalition"—began weeping and cheering, seemingly involuntarily, as Jackson's preaching began to roll over the vast assembly. And at that moment, it became clear to all that Jackson was no longer a candidate for the presidency. He had become, at that moment of his transition, a superordinate moral voice for the redress of the gross insensitivities of the Reagan Administration and the inadequacies of the federal polity. Such was the scale of that observable transition and the power of Jackson's recovery of the African-American performed sermon style in a national political context.

Impressions aside, at some point a closer examination of the Jackson speeches during his campaign for the American presidency is going to prove profitable and illuminating. Hopefully, this present work with its emphasis on the structure of the African-American sermon and its performance characteristics will facilitate that study.

To conclude, this work is about a way of life, or more accurately, a major narrative event in and around which millions of African-American lives move. I hope a by-product of this study is a new regard for the sermon and increased respect for the African-American preacher.

Chapter One

Finding the Wheat in the Chaff

Considerations in the Study of the
Performed African-American Sermon

Sundays at Ephesians Church of God in Christ are pretty much like
Sundays in any African-American church. At about 9:00 A.M., Sunday
school classes begin. At Ephesians, children and young people meet in
various areas of the basement. Sister Smith conducts adult classes for
women in the first pews on the left side of the sanctuary. The class for
men, which Bishop Cleveland sometimes attends as a class member,
takes place on the right side of the choir loft. And another class is held
in the sanctuary, midway on the right side, for mixed couples.

A bit after 10:00 A.M., the Sunday school classes break up. Choir
members move slowly to the robing area. The deacons begin to set up
the chancel area for the service, putting out the flowers, arranging the
chairs and the pulpit, setting out the trays for offering, and adjusting
the sound levels for the public address system. Bishop Cleveland goes
up to his office to don his robe for the day and to go over any last-
minute changes with Elder Luster and Elder Quinn, Cleveland's young
associate pastor.

At about 10:30 A.M., the choirs begin assembling in the vestibule
in the rear of the church. Members of the congregation who did not
attend Sunday school begin coming into the sanctuary to find their
seats. Women seem to predominate on the left side of the church; the
right side seems to have more men and young couples. The mothers of
the church begin moving into their reserved section at the left front of
the church just before the first-tier chancel railing, facing the congregation. The musicians occupy the area in front of the first-tier chancel
railing on the right side of the church.

At 10:45 A.M. or so, the Praise Service begins. Mrs. Sylvia Guiton,
the church's praise song leader, says that "the Praise Service is . . . al-

most as important as a minister. Because where a lot of people can't
relate to a message, they can certainly relate to singing." More to the
point, Mrs. Guiton says that the Praise Service "sets the pace for the
service." She continues, "It gives us an opportunity to express our
feelings to Christ for what He has done for us not just one day but the
whole week."[1]

The Praise Service may continue for anywhere from fifteen to
forty minutes with Mrs. Guiton lining-out hymns in her rich, elegant
voice with a bluesy gospel quality. The sometimes solo, sometimes congregational singing is interspersed with personal testimony and witnessing by members of the congregation. It is a powerful part of the
Sunday service, and it is Mrs. Guiton's role to "prepare the church" and
"raise the spirit." The Praise Service is closed by a prayer, usually led
by one of the deacons. There is a brief instrumental interlude by the
organist and the church rises to receive the choir.

Ushers open the double doors at the rear of the church and the
choir moves down the center aisle, singing, to the front of the church,
around the right side behind the musicians and into the choir loft. At
the same time, Elder Quinn and the senior deacons and pulpit guests
move through the door on the left side of the church and into the seats
on the first tier of the chancel.

Elder Quinn or the presiding deacon will usually have some remarks, and then there is a long prayer and a selection or two by the
choir, perhaps a Bible reading, and announcements from the pulpit and
the congregation. The presiding pastor or deacon will then prepare the
church to receive Bishop Cleveland, usually with an introduction such
as the one Elder Quinn spoke on February 11, 1981:

> I'm getting ready at this time to present to you a man of God
> He has received the name because of his traveling Globetrotter
> International evangelist
> Pastor and Bishop
> Saints, I want each of you to just look up to Jesus
> And reach out they faith and receive what God has in store for you
> I want everybody to give God a great big handclap as we present to you
>   BISHOP E. E. CLEVELAND!

Bishop Cleveland enters the sanctuary through the door on
the left, preceded by Elder Luster, and moves behind the pulpit. He
moves to the music of the band and the handclapping of the congregation. There are several "Amens!" from the congregation, and Bishop
Cleveland takes over the service.

On April 29, 1969, when Cleveland preached the key sermon

"You're Just Not Ready," several important events preceded the actual sermon performance. About one-third of the way through the service, Cleveland intoned a heavily formulaic prayer. The prayer was followed by a spirit-raising rendition of "There Is No Failure in God" sung by the Edwin Hawkins Singers and referred to by Cleveland in the opening moments of his sermon.[2] This was an especially crucial juncture in the development of the atmosphere in which the sermon was preached. In much the same way a teller of tales uses narrative devices and paralinguistic techniques to adjust his or her performance, so does the African-American preacher, or a surrogate, utilize a series of techniques and devices prior to mounting the pulpit for the sermon, for the purpose of "lining-up" his congregation.

The use of the phrase "lining-up" should not be taken to mean that African-American congregations can be browbeaten into predictable response patterns by a black-robed preacher-general. Rather, the term is intended to identify that portion of a congregation's energies that are voluntarily yielded to the preacher for the duration of the sermon. It is the preacher's task and duty to charge the preaching environment with dynamic energies and in so doing to induce the congregation to focus oral and aural mechanisms on the content and structure of the sermon performance. Preacher and congregation are locked into an aesthetic environment dependent on the continual transmission of messages between the units of the performing community for the successful realization of the performance. An African-American congregation listens attentively and critically to a sermon and can instantaneously withhold assent and response if a preacher fails to speak acceptably. Tradition merely offers a framework, a structure, and organizing principles for the dynamic performance of the African-American sermon.

Even before the sermon begins, then, Cleveland and his congregation have a sense of the depth of the interaction likely to take place during the preaching. If the spoken and sung preparatory modes have been successful, the congregation's aural-oral mechanisms have been developed into a sermonic counterpointing instrument capable of several levels of spiritual expression. If the preparatory modes are unsuccessful, the preacher will likely spend a substantial portion of the time he would customarily devote to the delivery of his message to "raising the spirit" of his "dead church."

Cleveland senses the appropriateness of his move into the pulpit. Waiting just long enough to permit the relative silence of the organ postlude (to the song sung by the Edwin Hawkins Singers) to settle the congregation, Bishop Cleveland begins his sermon: (see appendix for full text of sermon)

1 God bless you
    Everybody say Amen
    As I was walking up the street to church tonight
    Praying as I walked along
5 The Lord gave me this message
    And I didn't know what the choir was going to sing tonight
    But I wish you'd listen
    Isaiah, the fifty-ninth chapter said
    Behold,
10 The Lord's hands are not shortened
    That He cannot save
    Neither His ear heavy
    That He cannot hear
    But your iniquity has separated
15 Between you and your God
    And your sins have hid His face from you
    That He will not hear
    For your hands are defiled with blood
    Your fingers with iniquity
20 Your lips have spoken lies
    Your tongue have muttered perverseness
    None call for justice
    Nor any pleads for truth
    They trust in vanity
25 And speak lies
    They conceive mischief
    And bring forth iniquity.
    And you know what the Lord said?
    I want you to repeat after me
30 The fault
    Is not in the Lord
32 You are just not ready

In thirty-two lines, actually a miniformulaic introduction to the sermon and the first full sermon formulaic unit, Cleveland has accomplished the following:

1.   He has encouraged his congregation to respond, not at random, but at directed intervals (lines 2 and 29–32).
2.   He has identified the floating thematic bridges that have a displacement range equal to the length of the entire sermon—(*a*) "The fault ain't in Me (line 34)," and (*b*) "You are just not ready."[3]

3. He has established his basic chant-meter *sensibility*, and by so doing has provided his congregation with a shared sense of his mnemonic eurhythmic structure for the particular sermon performance.

4. He has identified the necessary abstracted sacred and "weighted secular" polarity and reinforced the polarity with a biblical text.

5. He has set up a verbal mold, or total sermon structure, as a narrative idea familiar to his congregation.

Essentially, in the first lines of his sermon, Cleveland has completed the first phase of the African-American sermon performance model. He has put before his congregation, in a coordinated framework, the syntactic and theological ideas and structures from which the full sermon performance will be generated. In addition to serving the functional purpose of promoting the interaction between the preacher and the congregation of the sermon performance, lines 29–32 are Cleveland's request for recognition that he has reached the first major threshold of the performance and for permission from the congregation to move forward into the development of the sermon proper. Understanding this, the congregation gives full assent to Cleveland's request for antiphonic approval and response.

Cleveland then begins cautiously to expand the sermon's theme, restating the sermon's thematic bridges and moving progressively to a demonstration of his own idiosyncratic style (lines 33–46). He is also preparing the congregation to move with him across the abstracted sacred/weighted secular threshold into a series of specific secular illustrations of the sermon theme. Cleveland begins with a careful, conservative interpretation of the biblical text:

33 God said here in Isaiah, the fifty-ninth chapter
   The fault ain't in Me [*thematic bridge (a)*]
35 I know you're just about to turn atheist
   You're just about to say there ain't no God
   You're just about to say I'm dead
   But the fault ain't in Me
   You're just not ready [*thematic bridge (b)*]
40 For My blessings
   Hallelujah to God
   Your iniquity have separated between you and your God
   And your sins have hid His face from you
   You speak lies and perverse things
45 Thank God
46 And it's because of you that you can't get the blessing

As the transition line from the sacred to the secular, line 46 is worth noting. Line 46 is the first indication of the syntactic use of multiple coding across ostensibly polarized and inviolable sacred/secular space. Through line 45, Cleveland has unmistakably represented his message and himself as the media through which the teachings are brought to his congregation. In line 46, however, that distinction becomes ambiguous. In fact, this is the threshold into secular example, and Cleveland appropriately assumes his own "voice" as the preacher, the leader of his flock, the guide of the faithful through the temptations of the world. Continuing the first formulaic unit, Cleveland fully assumes the mantle of the secular seer and guardian:

47   It doesn't mean that you can't get married now
      Plenty folks get married
      But everybody ain't ready to get married
      [*"why?" and "because" are understood here*]
50   You haven't got your blood test
      You haven't got your license
      You haven't got your divorce
      It's not final
      You got six more months to go
55   So you are not ready
      To get married
      And folks are getting married every day
58   Glory to God

Many African-Americans believe that if a person does not achieve his fullest potential it is because there are forces in nature supported by perverse forces in the society that act to restrict and restrain him or her. Those forces, some believe, are so overpowering that it is useless to combat them directly, and thus they justify "gaming" and "hustling" as social strategies. Cleveland takes exception to this rationalized behavior and explores the equally commonplace notion that men do control their fortunes in the United States and receive in proportion to their willingness to be gainfully, if not creatively, employed.

In three subformula sets, Cleveland explores this idea in three secular contexts. Initially, he identifies a job situation and the inability of African-American applicants to fill out employment forms. Next he spotlights the African-American who applies for college admission with a poor high school record and the knowledge that his application will likely be denied. In a summary set Cleveland catalogs the kinds of jobs which require little additional training for African-Americans and to which African-Americans have been limited by a racially discriminating American social system. He also renders judgment on the work of social workers, understood to mean African-Americans who are compromised by the values and structures of a racist America, acquired through college training.

Cleveland completes the first formula with a return to the sacred environment and the resumption of God's "voice." Thematic bridge (*b*) is used as a transition to the next formulaic unit.

> No, you're just not ready
> 85 Say, you take home economics
> You take agriculture
> You go take social work
> Go to asking folks how long they been on the welfare
> You are not ready
> 90 God said
> You just not ready
> For Me to answer your questions
> You are not ready
> 94 For me to give you your request

Juxtaposed against the series of preparations needed for success in the secular environment, success in the sacred environment is relatively simple. The petitioner merely has to make the decision to give himself to God. Unlike the major life decisions that require much of one's resources in the secular world, only a "low down payment" (line 113) is needed for success in the sacred world.

The second formulaic unit begins at this point; first it is in the abstracted sacred context, then it develops through specifically identified secular illustration. Line 97 indicates that for Cleveland, at least, the distinctions between sacred and secular references become unimportant. In what may be an idiosyncrasy, Cleveland introduces a secular intrusion into the sacred context.

> 95 If you get ready
> Man, in quicker than the flash of an eye
> I'll come when you call
> While you just preachin'
> I'll answer
> 100 My God
> Get ready
> You'll have to go with Me
> If you just decide
> I'll give you the size of your heart

105 But you got to be ready
     Oh, praise God
     Hallelujah
     Man say
     My God, come down and get what you want
110 Come down and get furniture
     Come down and get a car
     Come down, low down payment
     Come down and get all your vacation clothes
     And make a payment when you come back
115 Come down
     And a whole lot of folks can't go down there
117 Because they're not ready

The third formula deals with what can accrue to the person who
"gets ready," and also apprises the congregation of the pitfalls of empty
commitment. Bishop Cleveland uses the story of Joshua as an exemplum in this formula. God tells Joshua that as long as he is faithful
to God's laws he will win all of his battles. Someone in Joshua's com-
mand steals a gold idol. Joshua subsequently loses the major battle and
curses God.

184 God said, "Get up from here
     The fault ain't in Me
     There is a Babylonian god
     That's stolen back in the camp
     I can't work with nobody stealing
189 Say yeah
     You know you done told lies
     So don't get down and pray
192 You gonna be beating your gums for nothing"

Intensifying the message and moving to the nonsacred environment, Cleveland cites another exemplum, a narrative of a little boy in
Chicago who is visited by a nonbelieving friend. It is the custom of the
house that before the little boy goes to bed, he and any visiting friends
have to get on their knees in prayer. Instead of following the house custom, the little visitor queries:

215 Suppose there ain't nobody up there?
     And we just hollering up there for nothing?

The import, or the moral, of the exemplum is obvious to the congregation; the little visitor is "just not ready."

The sermon ends with a fourth formula concerned with how one "gets ready." In a reassuring formula that harmonizes the Christian life with the secular world, Cleveland offers a carrot for those who want both to "get ready" and keep one foot in the secular world.

219 A whole lot of folks done decided
    There's somebody up there
    Hallelujah
    You may not know it
    May not ever know it
224 But it's somebody up there
    But you just ain't ready for Him
    Yes
    He just ain't ready to answer
    My God
    Hallelujah to God
230 And so when you go to criticize and
    Say there's nothing to it
    And God don't answer prayer
    And these folks are lying when they say God give them this
    And that God give them that
235 Before you do that
    You get ready
    Before you get caught
    Because He said
    If you get ready
240 Ask what you will
    And it shall be granted
    If you believe what you praying
    [unclear]
    Bible say, How you gonna believe?
245 Say well, He's Jesus of Nazareth
    You just not ready
    And how I'm gonna get ready Brother Cleveland?
    Repent of your sins
    How do I repent Brother Cleveland?
250 Acknowledge your sins
    Confess your sins and forsake them
    Let the wicked forsake his way
    An unrighteous man his thoughts
    And let him come unto the Lord
255 And He'll have mercy upon him

And will verily pardon him
My God
If the people that's powerful
Would proffer themselves
260   And pray
And seek My faith
And turn from their wicked ways
Then they will hear from Him
[*unclear*]
265   The Scriptures say
Ain't willing to give up
Ain't willing to give up the LSD
Ain't willing to give up the marijuana
Ain't willing to give up they hatred
270   Ain't willing to give up they strife
Ain't willing to give up they cars
Put yourself in the right hand of God
And He will raise you up
274   God resents the powerful and gives grace to the humble

Cleveland completes the sermon with a heavily formulaic prayer. Characteristically, the prayer is to guide people as they strive to realize a dedicated life among the temptations of a secular existence.

In light of this examination of the Cleveland key sermon, I am bound to refer to an opinion offered by Daniel Crowley that "there is very little logical progression in the preaching." Rosenberg is more appreciative of the skills of the preacher, although he also would seem to minimize the control a preacher has over his form. It is abundantly clear, however, that both Rosenberg and Crowley underestimate the mechanics of African-American sermonic technique. Once a preacher has established his meter and his request for antiphonic response has been met by his congregation, the preacher's primary concern shifts to the structure and content of his sermon theme. Meter and antiphony become subordinated mnemonic devices. After establishing the parameters of his "turf," the African-American preacher becomes Roger Abrahams's "man-of-words," a sermon songster.[4]

Rosenberg argues that "the oral preacher subordinates everything he has to say to the demands of his meter."[5] Seeming to support Rosenberg, and assuming his notion of "timing" is approximately the same as Rosenberg's "meter," Mitchell writes:

Good storytelling . . . biblical or nonbiblical, requires a sense of timing. The teller must give enough details and action to keep the story moving

and compel action. Yet, he must also measure his pace so that the story
is understood and the hearer stays abreast of the action in his identification with the narrative. This is especially true in the Black sermon. . . .
Black Bible stories are to be relived, not merely heard. This requires a
certain expertise in timing and emphasis so that attention is not dis-
tracted on the one hand by the effort to keep up or by boredom on the
other.[6]

Rosenberg's notion of meter is literary and is based on phrasings
which are consistently and regularly patterned. The minimal African-
American sermonic phrase is highly irregular when reduced to print,
but it is made regular and *seemingly* metrical *in performance* through
the use of music and sound production principles.

Mitchell's commentary on the use of tone by Black preachers is an
interesting point of departure in this discussion:

In addition to mannerisms Black preachers abound in other stylistic
features. The most common or stereotypical is the use of a musical
tone or chant in preaching. Among the initiates it is variously referred
to as "moaning," "mourning," "whooping," "turning," "zooming," or
any of several other terms, each with a slightly different shade of meaning. . . . Sustained tone is used in various ways. Some Black preachers
use it only in climatic utterance, of whatever length. Others, often less
well-educated and therefore less inhibited, tend to use some degree of
tone throughout the message. Still others use it only in places where
the . . . congregation demands it. The decision will often be made
unconsciously.[7]

Certainly one would want to quarrel with Mitchell's conviction that the
expansive use of tone by African-American preachers is the result of
the uninhibited behavior made possible by the minimal interference of
behavior-modifying American education. There are simply too many
well-educated African-American preachers who use a wide variety of
affective, expressive devices and techniques in their preaching, including the variety of affect Mitchell refers to as "tone," to permit this observation to go unchallenged. But the thrust of Mitchell's commentary
should not be missed. African-American culture is still dynamically
oral. While literary precepts and conventions are useful in framing approaches to the examination of the expressive products of oral cultures, in the final analysis the scholar interested in these areas must
look directly at the expressive systems for the answers he or she desires.

The foregoing first-level analysis of Cleveland's sermon "You're Just
Not Ready" demonstrates most of those characteristics, the "logic,"
and the structure of the African-American performed sermon. Also
demonstrated are the consistent development of theme and theological

polarities maintained in the performance of the sermon by African-American preachers. Together, these factors establish the complexity and narrative techniques of African-American sermon performance.

The Aesthetics of African-American Sermon Performance

African-American narrative performance is guided by concepts of *ideal* forms and *ideal* standards. The notion of an ideal form is as compelling for the African-American performer as it is for his or her audience. During a performance, when both "performer" and "audience" are actively locked into a dynamic exchange, the audience compels the performer to acknowledge the most appropriate characteristics of the genre system—the "ideal" in terms of that particular performance environment—before permitting the performer sufficient latitude for the individuation of his genius and style. It is the mechanics of this dynamic exchange between the units of the African-American performing context—performer, audience, performing mode—that encourages this discussion of the aesthetic (valuational) dimensions in African-American sermon performance.

In a general commentary on the performance of oral materials, Robert Kellogg provides support for the view outlined above of the nature of the narrative performer's styles. The performer in oral tradition, he says, "makes every attempt to conform his performance, in style, in form, and in content to a tradition that already exists in his mind and in the mind of his audience. His performance, in other words, is an attempt to re-experience a thing that already exists in some ideal way in tradition."[8] Kellogg's postulation of ideal forms in folk narrative performance is not intended to proximate literary ideas of prototypic or original forms of a generic system. Tradition, for Kellogg, is more akin to the customary, rationalized, and dynamic usage of folk ideational structures in performance than to fixed historically generated forms slavishly reproduced for an audience by an untalented folk narrator.

The preceding distinction is important because the African-American narrator, or narrative performer, is not generally concerned with aligning his performance against an original model that may have existed *in time*. His is not a quest for the recreation of the circumstances and form of the "first" performance of the genre. Indeed, the demands of the African-American audience for virtuosity and dynamic invention in the performance of a recognized form precludes the performer's adherence to the static reproduction of familiar and popular narrative forms.

There are exceptions. The exceptions occur most frequently where narrative systems carry highly specialized functions. These exceptions are sufficiently commonplace to render Lord's observation that "in oral tradition the idea of an original is illogical" somewhat inappropriate to segments of African diasporic narrative materials.[9] For some performers of oral tradition, the perpetuation of the *sense* of an original is both logical and desirable. In societies and cultures in which historical data substantially represent the life-defining circumstances of the group, the oral narrator must be able to recite and recreate the group's history with unerring fidelity to the "original" events. While the narrator-historian has license to embellish his reports of events with gestures and other paralinguistic systems, the narrative itself is not expected to differ in word or phrase from what has been previously understood to be the "original." But these are the exceptions.

Folk narrative performance in African-American communities is dynamic and inventive. The responsibility for engaging and manipulating the several components of the African-American performance environment is not the performer's alone, however. The several responsibilities and obligations to realize the most effective, consistent, and innovative "reading" of a narrative event are shared by audience and performer. There are few *passive tradition bearers* in an African-American performing context and the *active tradition bearers*—those who perform—are not thought of as solo virtuosi.[10] For example, African-American preachers commonly admonish their congregation that they can't "preach to no dead church," a church in which the presence of the spirit is not made manifest by active vocal response to "the Word" as represented in the preached sermon. Popular performers will frequently go to extraordinary lengths to exhort an audience to clap hands or join the performance by singing along or shouting "Amen!" in reply to a performer's quasi-churched solicitation. At times this needed interaction is even more direct. Performers will invite or pull members of the audience to the performing platform as if to blur completely the distinctions that separate performer from audience in Euro-American performance contexts. This is apt to be most evident in a performance in an arena that does not encourage intimacy and feedback, or when the African-American performer desires a particular kind of reinforcement from quieted African-Americans in a largely non–African-American audience. This relationship between an African-American performer, his African-American audience, and the ideal and realized performed narrative event is schematized in figure 1.

The circularity, or spiraling, in figure 1 is purposeful. However African-American performance and creativity might be observed, the

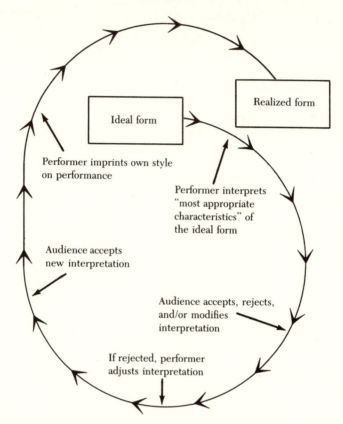

FIGURE 1.   Diagram of African-American validation model

organizing principle of circularity, rather than linearity, is evident. While this organizing principle of cultural performance may be present in other ethnic and racial communities, it holds a central, core importance in African-American performance.[11] Linearity is most commonly associated with the organization of Anglo-European cultural performance.[12]

In its most literal sense, the notion of circularity appears in African-American pulpit and podium performance. "What goes around, comes around," is a retribution maxim that reached a new popularity in the months following the Watergate disclosures. The African-American politician or preacher would at some appropriate point in his performance intone "what goes around—" and the audience or congregation would conclude with the phrase "comes around." The metaphonic performance of this well-known folk aphorism in which both audience and performer participated, would be acknowledged by a great deal of head-shaking, heavy "amens," or laughter, appropriate to the occasion.

The circularity in this aphorism is not simply carried by the inclusion of the word "around," however. There is a greater cosmological sense that the process of retribution is a balance sheet tallied in the universe. Nixon did not get what *he* deserved; he symbolically represented the correcting of an imbalance that was historical. Malcolm X's comment on John Kennedy's assassination that "chickens were coming home to roost"—a comment that resulted in his suspension from the Nation of Islam—was not necessarily an observation on Kennedy's participation in covert wrongdoings. Rather, he was commenting on the militaristic, colonialistic appetite of the United States government.

Circularity as an organizing principle of an African-American performance can also be observed in environments that are more familiar to performance categorizations. African-American popular music, improvisation music or jazz, preaching, some forms of dance, and even selected material culture forms exhibit manifestations of circular performance organization. That is, each of these forms exhibits circular organizational structures sufficiently similar to the others to suggest a shared aesthetic foundation or sensibility among African-Americans.

Structurally, the circularity principle operates as follows. There is an initial statement, a motif or core element, in which all of the characteristics of the ideal form of the event are concentrated. In music this statement can be a sentiment expressed in the lyric or a phrase in the music itself, or a combination of both. In dance, the core element can be a basic series of movements, or a foundation pattern, that is elaborated as the dance progresses. In preaching, this motif is frequently a sound phrase or semantic phrase strategically repeated for semantic or stylistic purposes. In material culture, basket making for instance, the foundation is the particular, careful, articulated joining of the materials at the center of the creative event. The "motif" is the most basic form of the event and contains all of the information the audience needs to permit the performer to move into what is oftentimes idiosyncratic development of the ideal form. Once the motif is identified, the performer is "released" by the audience to establish the *realized* form of the event.

At successive stages, the performer becomes increasingly innovative, though he is bound to return to the original statement, the motif, at regular intervals. Finally, with the approbation of the audience, expressed verbally or with handclapping, the performer is permitted to range freely. Often the motif is inverted or discarded altogether at this stage, but before terminating the motif, the performer will restate it. The "final statement" or resolution in terms of the performance is rarely "permanent." It is very much in the nature of the circular organization of African-American performance that the resolution must seem related to temporal circumstances beyond the most immediate range of the performed event. It is this thrust beyond the immediate circumstances of the performance that gives African-American performance, generally, its dynamic, deathless character.

But what is most critical is not the *how* of African-American performance, but rather how performance ideas and standards, including performance structures, are maintained. Two propositions are suggested in this regard:

1. The notion of an African-American "mind" is a legitimate intellectual construct for observing the implications of African-American ideal and realized forms and standards in performance.

2. An identifiable African-American aesthetic system, or systems, including valuation, supports the generation and maintenance of ideal forms and standards in African-American folk and popular performance.

Kellogg provides a useful framework for the examination of these propositions with his consideration of the traditional performer's inclination to conform his performance to meet existing ideas in the mind of his audience, and with his suggestion of "tradition" as the watershed for a community's notions of ideal forms and standards.

It was stated earlier that there were two active components in the maintenance of performance standards and forms for African-American materials: the performer and the audience. There is, as well, a third component. That component is tradition, or *characteristic* customary, habitual, and dynamic employment of folk ideas in a performance context.

The shared responsibility between the performer and his or her audience in the context of the performed narrative event is not casual and seems to follow well-defined sets of compacts. These compacts have historical implications even though most African-American narrative performers manifest what George Kent calls "isness," the power of contemporaneity in performance.[13] So consistently are the patterns of agreements evidenced in performance that those who participate in any given performance—audience and performer—can be considered to participate in an aesthetic community. Elsewhere I have defined "aesthetic community" as "a group of people sharing the knowledge for the development and maintenance of a particular affecting mode or 'craft' and the articulating principles to which the affecting mode must adhere or oppose [in performance]. Both conditions, articulated in and evidenced in the mode itself, must be present."[14]

The aesthetic community concept assumes the existence of an established cultural community having the capacity to identify the forms and types of its cultural products—Robert Armstrong's "affecting things and events."[15] Particularly, the salient organizing principles of the community's expressive products will share cross-generic factors articulated by the community through the cultural mechanisms of generic interlock and generic complementarity. Further, the aesthetic community regularly employs the processes and systems that support and determine the form and shape of the affecting modes native to the culture, and it has identified which of its affecting modes will be available to modifying influences by forces and events external to the community. Obviously the principles, systems, and processes that support a community's cultural affecting modes and the regulating community of participants to which the modes "belong" are not static. They are always in dynamic process, evaluating, accepting, or discarding modal elements. A final note which must be obvious, as in Dundes's definition of folk groups,[16] a person may belong to several aesthetic communities, though one will tend to predominate and give character to the others, presumably one's racial or ethnic community.

The success of the aesthetic community concept rests on a successful articulation of aesthetics as an African-American performance valuation system. My use of aesthetics is derived from the Greek verb *aisthanesthai*, meaning to feel or perceive through the senses.[17] Armstrong's conceptualization of "affecting things and events" as "these objects and happenings in any given culture . . . accepted by those native to that culture as being purposefully concerned with potency, emotion, values and states of being or experience . . . —all, in a clear sense, powers" is useful here as well.[18] Most immediately, the statements help to shift the defining ground of aesthetics away from professional philosophers, who are preoccupied with generating ontologic categories of creative perfection, to people and communities known as the folk, for whom decisions about the quality of performances are an everyday commonplace.

African-Americans render judgments on performance of African-American materials. Those judgments are made from a consistent valuational base. I am attempting here to identify the components of that base and to reconstruct a valuation system based on African-Americans' judgments of the quality of performed events.

Stephen Henderson and Addison Gayle, among several others, have begun to explore questions of aesthetics in African-American literature. So far, Henderson alone seems to exhibit the excellence of perception, the knowledge of the materials, and African-American inventiveness generally, to get a firm handle on the investigation. But folk materials present a different set of problems from those encountered in investigations of aesthetics in the development of relatively fixed forms. Even George Kent's elegant and concise notion of "sensibility"—in fact, a definition of African-American aesthetic valuation—is limited to artists who work in literary genres. "By the term sensibility," writes Kent, "I mean the writer's means of sensing, apprehending, his characteristic emotional, psychic, and intellectual response to existence." Kent's "sensibility" has a passive and *seeming* spontaneous invention that characterizes many of the materials and systems of African-American folklore.[19]

What I am looking for is a set of categories that anticipate and embrace action and power in the creation of African-American folklore materials. What I am seeking quite precisely is the identification of those qualities and considerations that are actively manipulated by participants in African-American performing environments that result in the identification of an "ideal" narrative structure and the production of a "realized" form. Armstrong's notion of "power" and the following considerations are especially appropriate in this regard:

1. "Potency, emotion, values, and (the) recognition of states of being or experience" (Armstrong's "powers"),[20] are generating motives in African-American folklore performance

2. Although a considerable amount of the information manifest in a performance environment is perceived sensually and via sensibility mechanisms by African-Americans, the most important aspect of this process is the organization of those perceptions into a systematic, codified series of expressive responses

3. The balance, in the performance of African-American folklore events and systems, between tradition (customary, habitual, and dynamic usage of folk ideas in performance) as a structural framework and contemporaneity (Kent's "is-ness") is a shaping force internal to the performed event or system

In the following chapter, the balance consideration is characterized as a sacred/secular tension. These pairings, traditional/contemporaneity and sacred/secular, seem to be contrapositional sets. They are, in fact, synchronous polarities in the shaping of African-American folklore performance. Even the circular organizing principle written of earlier can be thought of as a spiral. That is, the head or beginning of the performed event does not find its tail as if terminating the performance. More frequently, the resolution of the event seems to take place in a temporal space beyond that which is occupied by the performed event, the performer, and the audience. The illustrative point of this is obvious in the church context, where it is understood by all participants that the weight of a well-preached sermon is to be carried into areas of life beyond the temporal and physical space occupied by the performance of the sermon. It is not so obvious when one considers more conventional performance situations. For this purpose any performance by African-American popular performers James Brown or Little Richard is illustrative. At the close of the performance, both performers, exhausted and weary, turn toward the wings and start to exit. Then, as if taken by an invisible force, the performer is "pulled" to center stage and sings a few additional bars and attempts to leave the stage once more. Again, as if pulled by some external force, the singer returns to stage center, sings, and attempts to leave. The action may be repeated any number of times. However, with each repetition of the cycle some new movement is added. A towel may be given to the performer by an attendant or he may simply resume center stage and do a holy dance, as Little Richard did, or the performer may start to slump to the floor. Finally, an attendant comes on stage with a cloak and removes the now totally exhausted performer, who may in one final gesture fling off the cloak and return to center stage, there to be recloaked by the indulgent attendant and led from the stage. For the audience, this is a powerful, gripping experience; no less so for the performer. Both have experienced a fusion between a spiritually perceived generating force and the power and insistent demands of contemporary virtuosity. The power of the performance moves well beyond the walls of the auditorium or the church. As in the church, the spiritual essence, the cosmological value of the performance may well be carried into the days and weeks following the actual performance as those who experienced the performance, or those who have heard reports of the performance, discuss it, evaluate it, and relive it.

The performer has restated traditional ideas and exercised idiosyncratic invention. That is, he has initially identified an ideal form, offered it to his audience, interpreted their response, made any required adjustments, then proceeded to establish the power of his own genius in the expansion of the ideal form to its fullest, most appropriate realized form.

Because the intent is always to focus on the expressive act as the pivotal consideration in the definition of the African-American sermon, the use of the term "performance" is significant. The intention is to find a term that embraces a variety of related concepts which merge in the preached sermon event. Some of these concepts are similar to the elements Richard Bauman identifies in his equation of performance with modes of artistic speech. In his article "Verbal Arts as Performance," Bauman sets his equation in the context of contemporary folkloristics:

> In a recent collection of conceptual and theoretical essays in folklore, assembled to indicate a range of new perspectives in the field, it was emphasized in the Introduction that the contributors showed a common concern with performance as an organizing principle. The term performance was employed there . . . because it conveyed a dual sense of artistic *action*—the doing of folklore—and the artistic *event*—the performance situation, involving performer, art form, audience, and setting—both of which are central to the developing performance approach to folklore.[21]

One of the consequences of the use of the performance concept in the present work is a shift of focus from the preacher—the performer of sermons—to the performed sermon as event. The preacher is obviously an important personality in any consideration of the sermon genre.[22] And as a practical matter, the performed sermon embraces a number of elements, many of which are under the control of the preacher. But my concern here is the identification of as many of the sermon's constituent elements as possible, and the provision of a rationale for the use and manipulation of these elements in the performed sermon context. This concept, the sermon as event, is an extension of Dell Hymes's speech event categories and includes, in addition to the sender-performer, "his audience, the style of his message, the code he is using, his topic, the scene of his communication."[23] In such a configuration the preacher is obviously important. But the identification and exploration of certain African-American aesthetic principles and the structures of the African-American sermon are more immediate priorities.

It is not desirable to explore the structures of the sermon as event without a careful consideration of the sermon as a narrative system.

The sermon is an organic body which derives its dynamic properties from smaller, coordinated working units. The sermon is, in this respect, a system. The systemic, integrated aspects of the sermon event, and the functioning smaller sermon units form the content of this study. To facilitate the examination of the relationships between event, system, and systemic elements, a dyadic methodological framework has been developed.

The text, those linguistically identifiable idiosemantic hemistich phrases that when taken as a whole comprise the sermon, provides the principal mechanism for the analyses of the African-American sermon. Text study yields information on phrase structures, narrative technique, word and thought organization, and a series of related analytic categories which carry integral functions.

The other principal concern is an examination of the interior structures of the African-American sermon and the units of which the sermon system is constructed. Methodologically, this focus groups compatible, contiguous phrases (sermon lines) into narrative units that embrace either a single thought or a single purpose or function. The functions of a sermon unit are distinguished by elaboration and illustration and by advancement of the narrative or homiletic action of the sermon.

Fitting the functions of the sermon units into a model of the genre is an important part of the analytic enterprise. The sermons used in this study were intentionally drawn from preachers of differing styles and theological backgrounds. The model is, however, not a conflation of the components of several sermons. Rather the model is derived from the study of one sermon selected from the collected corpus. The preacher of the sermon, Bishop Cleveland, is not necessarily the "best" preacher. His sermon, however, is exemplary. Any African-American sermon ought to be recognizable when evaluated alongside the African-American sermon model generated from the study of Cleveland's "You're Just Not Ready." Any substantial deviation from the sermon model, as frequently occurs, permits the analyst to make additional determinations about the nature of creativity and tradition in the preaching event.

A secondary concern of this study is how best to use the information resulting from a structural analytic approach in a way that is supportive of broader theoretical applications. For instance, there are large areas of similarity and overlap in the performance of some narrative systems in African-American communities and in the responses accorded the performance of these systems by African-American people. In some cases performers of seemingly unrelated and oftentimes antithetic expressive systems—"antithetic" at least in the literature—and modes are the same personalities.[24]

One direct result of this line of inquiry is the discovery of a unified body of performance rules and characteristics which support the performance of sermons, blues, political speech, and other genres in African-American contexts.

Zora Neale Hurston provides a succinct summary for this discussion of aesthetics among African-Americans. Hurston writes:

> Beneath the seeming informality of religious worship there is a set formality. Sermons, prayers, moans and testimonies have their definite forms. The individual may hang as many new ornaments upon the traditional form as he likes, but the audience would be disagreeably surprised if the form were abandoned. Any new and original elaboration is welcomed, however, and this brings out the fact that all religious expression among Negroes is regarded as art, and ability is recognized as definitely as in any other art. The beautiful prayer receives the accolade as well as the beautiful song. It is merely a form of expression which people generally are not accustomed to think of as art.[25]

Hurston's eloquence notwithstanding, we are still left the task of identifying some of the mechanics of African-American aesthetic invention. A structuralist approach is useful but probably can be justified only if it successfully generates for the sermon a genre definition that embraces social context, purpose (or intentionality), and creativity, as well as form and structure. Finally, we must scrutinize more closely the principles, which are recoverable, of African-American aesthetic valuation.

Generic interlock and generic complementarity are discussed more fully as cultural mechanisms in a later chapter.[26] Here I have laid the groundwork for the later discussion.

In his article "Expressive Profile," Brian Sutton-Smith advocates the use of generic complementarity in the analysis of folklore materials.

> By expressive forms it is meant that there are . . . ways of presenting or representing human experience, sufficiently consistent across individuals to permit functional and formal analyses. Given such unity, then, it might follow that analyses appropriate to one form would be illuminating when applied to another, or again, that within the experience of a given individual or group the forms may function in related or perhaps complementary ways.[27]

For French structuralists, interest in generic complementarity often takes the form of identifying the generating locus of a culture's philosophical systems; Levi-Strauss's *The Raw and the Cooked* is an excellent example. Dundes coined the term "metafolklore" to identify "folkloristic commentary about folklore genres."[28] The Dundes concept suggests that folk categories have an internal analytical capability. A further extension of the metafolklore concept provides for the identification of shared and exchanged generic functions, or generic complementarity, in a group's folklore systems. Such an extension also supports the identification of mechanisms for exchanging components of folklore items across generic boundaries, or generic interlock, as well.

Ben-Amos offers a more restrained entry into the folk taxonomy and generic classification discussion. He writes that folk taxonomic systems represent the "conception a culture has of its own folkloric communication as it is represented in the distinction of forms, the attribution of names to them, and the sense of the social appropriateness of their application in various cultural situations." Ben-Amos also notes that cultural events are often recorded in at least two of a culture's folklore systems, an observation shared by Sutton-Smith.[29]

William Bascom has demonstrated the strong complementarity between sculpture and legend in Yoruba cultural systems.[30] In a critique of modern painting, Merleau-Ponty offers a view similar to that of Bascom's, although Merleau-Ponty's view is more appropriate to the artist and visual materials than to folk communities and groups and verbal expression:

> Anyone who thinks about the matter finds it astonishing that very often a good painter can also make good drawings or good sculpture. Since neither the means of expression nor the creative gestures are comparable, this fact [of competence in several media] is proof that there is a system of equivalences, a logos of lines, of lighting, of colors, of reliefs, of masses, of concepts. . . . The effort of modern painting has been directed . . . toward multiplying the system of equivalences.[31]

Both Bascom and Merleau-Ponty evidence a heuristic concern for the existence of complementarity and interlock in the production of cultural expressive systems. And both men illustrate the co-occurrence of shared creative characteristics in at least two of a particular group's aesthetic expressive systems.

The literature provides support for the continued examination of group-employed cultural mechanisms. The real evidence, of course, lies in the commonplace occurrence of these mechanisms in daily communication forms. Generic interlock and generic complementarity are but two of those mechanisms, although the two which are most useful in this study.

Increasingly, folklorists want to know more about group categorizations of folklore materials and ethnoscience aspects of cultural organization. Much of this interest in the internal consistencies and philosophic principles underpinning the use of folklore as systems among groups of peoples is owing to the increasingly sophisticated applications of folkloristics. And much of the impetus for this research is attributable to the impact that native scholars studying materials peculiar to their own backgrounds and nonnative but affiliated scholars through strong partisanship in research and publication have had on the traditional presumptions of folklore, anthropology, and sociology.

Students of African-American folklore have been beneficiaries of the intense research described above. In some cases, contemporary research by African-American and non–African-American researchers continues interests and explorations begun years earlier; frequently contemporary scholars have broken new ground in African-American cultural research.

INTERPRETATIONS OF AFRICAN-AMERICAN PREACHING

American folklorists, anthropologists, and sociologists have long been familiar with the sermon in African-American religion. Many have commented on the genre's rich poetic meter or the "emotional" nature of the sermon in performance. Melville Herskovits wrote of the "intensified rhythmic effects" of the sermon. The African-American scholar William Pipes noted that "logical argument [in preaching] is not as important as emotional appeal. There is no logical organization because there is little preparation. The emotions determine everything." Pipes observed that the preacher only assumes an appearance of being logical, "certainly these ministers are entirely unaware of the classical works on logic." Daniel Crowley, writing some years after Pipes, concludes a brief passage with the following observations: "There is very little logical progression in the 'preaching.' Its function is to play upon the emotions of the hearers by means of elegant phrases and a rhythmical style." By concentrating on the affective characteristics of African-American preaching, scholars have obscured many of the structural considerations to be found in the African-American sermon event.[32]

Some scholars, such as Bruce Rosenberg, have made valuable, perceptive contemporary contributions to the study of African-American sermonry. At an earlier point in his career, Rosenberg was concerned with "learning something about spontaneous verse composition in the 14th Century."[33] But stimulated by Albert Lord's *The Singer of Tales*, Rosenberg subsequently defined his interest in spontaneous verse composition in the "illiteratures" of the African-American community—the performed sermon—the subject of his well-regarded *The Art of the American Folk Preacher*.[34] Rosenberg's focus, however, remains on the literary works so familiar to Classics scholars. Rosenberg describes his principal concern in the following manner:

> The tradition of which I have been speaking . . . is both vigorous and available. Few of us are inconveniently distant from its carriers. From these Americans [African-American preachers] we can learn much about the nature of oral literature and its composition, and perhaps discover something about Homer and the poet of *Beowulf*. The American singers of sermons are far more accessible than the guslars ever were, and have the advantage . . . of performing in English. It does not matter to our understanding of the principles of oral composition whether the singer repeats "that was a good king" or "let me tell you brother." The structure of the language, and not its semantics is the present concern. These Americans may one day enable us to understand remote and exotic literatures more thoroughly; patristic exegesis aside, Rev. Lacy may one day be able to tell us something about the composition of *Beowulf*.[35]

Rev. Mr. Lacy has enough to do without shouldering the responsibilities of Classics scholars, but Rosenberg's work in the study of the African-American sermon is exemplary and deserving of further, careful evaluation.

As recently as 1971, Rosenberg was still defensive about his folk sermon studies and appropriately critical of the meager attention scholars have paid the genre: "It is probably still necessary to defend an academic interest in and a scholarly journal's allotment of space to essays on the American folk sermon. . . . Lack of interest is in itself expressive of the disdain in which this religious mode is often held; consequently, few folk sermons have ever been published."[36] Rosenberg's contention is well founded. When the genre has been reported in the literature it has been treated summarily, rather as the bastard stepchild in a blue-veined family of familiar narrative genres. But where the study of the folk sermon in general has suffered from benign neglect, the study of the African-American sermon has suffered a characteristically different fate. Few scholars who have looked at the African-American sermon have fully appreciated the complexity of the structures of the performed African-American sermon. As a consequence the African-American sermon has been underestimated and underreported more than it has been held in disdain or neglected. Even the three most significant studies to date of the African-American sermon and the sermon performer—J. Mason Brewer's 1953 work on preacher tales, Rosenberg's 1970 study of the oral formulaic character of the "American" folk sermon, and Henry Mitchell's 1970 examination of the several contexts of Black preaching—do not treat the performed African-American sermon as a unified system of sociosemantic structures. Although Herskovits, Powdermaker, Johnson, Frazier, and Mays and Nicholson, all include chapters on African-American religion in their several studies, the sermon is handled only descriptively.[37]

Ironically, the line that concludes the Rosenberg quotation above —"few folk sermons have ever been published"—is evidence itself of the underestimation of the African-American sermon. Rosenberg would have been accurate to observe that few published sermons have entered the scholarly literature. The archival collections of African-Americana held in the libraries of Fisk and Howard Universities and other African-American institutions, in the Library of Congress, and in the New York Public Library and other municipal and university libraries around the nation include a number of significant and historically important sermons "published" by African-American preachers or their congregations. If the items in the Special Negro Archives and Manuscripts Collections of Fisk University and the Springarn-Moorland Collections of Howard University are representative, it would appear that even the most humble African-American church found the occasion to publish one or a set of sermons, frequently on the occasion of an anniversary.[38]

Doubtless, Rosenberg is making reference to the conventional scholarly literature when he mentions publication as a criterion for the respect held for the folk sermon. The notion of publishing is more broadly interpreted in this discussion and includes duplication of sermons by small churches intended for distribution to the congregations only. Although scholars did not take the sermon seriously, congregations obviously did. The printed versions were oftentimes fragmentary and devoid of affective notation, the result in some cases of heavy editing to bring the printed versions into comformity with the prevailing conventions of whatever church circulated the texts. Whether by reason of occasion, the excellence of a sermon, or status, African-American congregations and African-American preachers frequently elected to publish sermons. Many of those published sermons found their way to the archives of the nation's African-American universities. The practice continues currently and it is now commonplace for preachers and churches to tape record sermons and church services. Some larger urban churches have even installed elaborate videotape recording systems.

The high emotionalism of the African-American church has seemed to be especially problematical for scholars. It is probably one of the major reasons for the underreporting of the African-American sermon.

African-American scholars William Pipes and Lawrence Davis equate
affective preaching and affective responses to preaching, by African-
Americans, with lack of sophistication and education.[39] Pipes and Davis
reason that rationality is inversely proportional to the presence of
emotionalism in the church and the academic training of the preacher.
That is, the presence of emotionalism in the church precludes a concurrent ability to be rational and dispassionately evaluative. Curiously,
Daniel Crowley, writing some fifteen years after Pipes, also concludes
that the nature of African-American pulpit style is primitive. The sole
function of "preaching" argues Crowley, "is to play upon the emotions
of the hearers."[40]

Other aspects of this problematical area are manifested by Rosenberg and Elizabeth Kilham in articles written one hundred years apart.
In a 1970 article defining the folk sermon as a genre, Rosenberg asserts
that one of the reasons why the sermon is not well regarded is the low
esteem in which it is held by the folk. He suggests that the decrease in
the popularity of the African-American sermon over the last hundred
years is a direct result of the increase in educational opportunities for
African-Americans. He writes, "Many of 'Das Volk' themselves have
for over a century held the genre in low esteem, and the responses of
educated men and women have hardly been more tolerant."[41] To provide a historical dimension for this finding, Rosenberg cites an 1870
Putnam's Monthly article by Kilham:

> The distinctive features of Negro hymnology are gradually disappearing,
> and with another generation will probably be obliterated entirely. The
> cause for this lies in the education of the younger people. With increas-
> ing knowledge, comes growing appreciation of fitness and propriety, in
> this as in everything else; *and already they have learned to ridicule the
> extravagant preaching, the meaningless hymns, and the noisy singing of
> their elders* [emphasis added].[42]

It is not necessary to look beyond any African-American community in the United States, or in this hemisphere for that matter, to
discover the events which belie this series of "findings." Far from dis-
appearing from African-American communities, affective or emotive
worship is enjoying a radically ascending popularity. Even those congregations which count among their members well-educated, professional and middle-level management African-Americans are insisting
on preachers who are both learned and affective in their preaching.
Rev. Dr. Wyatt Tee Walker of Canaan Baptist Church in New York is a
superb example. Walker is scholarly, dynamic, economically astute,
and well grounded in the traditions of affective preaching. He is not

atypical. Even the ridicule of "extravagant preaching" of which Kilham complains and which Rosenberg reinterprets in his remarks, speaks of the vitality of the affective tradition in African-American cultural systems and the strength of the influence of the African-American preacher in the acquisition of verbal art skills by African-American young people. That is, what Kilham identifies as the signal of the demise of affective rhetorical style and response in the African-American church, Abrahams correctly sees as the most critical step in the development of the "man-of-words."

The purpose of this discussion is not simply to observe that some scholars misinterpret the African-American sermon. Rather, I am identifying an insidious process that seems endemic to American scholarship and teaching. Why does Rosenberg, who certainly knows of the vigor and vitality of the African-American church, feel compelled to assert the death of affective preaching, in contradiction to his research? How is it that Davis and Pipes, who spent their early lives in the African-American church, can dismiss affective church worship as purely emotional behavior of "unsophisticated Negroes"? How can Crowley's long-acknowledged respect for Caribbean folk materials be rationalized alongside a conclusion that "preaching" in African-American churches is rhetorically primitive?

One possible explanation lies in the circulation, in scholarship, of certain pseudotheoretical notions that are so pervasive and powerful— if only by their continued repetition—that they have the strength to alter empirically derived or intuitively felt intelligence and knowledge. One of these notions is what Dundes refers to as the "devolutionary-evolutionary premise" in folklore research and folkloric analysis.

> The gloomy reports of the death of Folklore are in part a result of the misguided and narrow concept of the folk as the illiterate in a literate society. . . . In essence, the idea is that the more education, especially the more literacy, the less the illiteracy and thus the less the number of folk and the less the folklore. . . . As nonliterate and illiterate man becomes literate, he will tend to lose his folklore.[43]

The premise Dundes identifies is clearly a compelling "truth" for the scholars mentioned previously. Rosenberg describes African-American sermons as "illiteratures." He suggests that the study of this material is important not of itself but in what Americans can learn about "other remote and exotic literatures." States Rosenberg, "Rev. Lacy may one day be able to tell us something about the composition of *Beowulf*."[44] The question of whether the incidence of the devolutionary-evolutionary premise distorts Rosenberg's examination of the oral formulaic character of the folk sermon is considered in chapter 3. The present discussion is intended only to illustrate a concern that many of the conventional ideas used in scholarly research reporting, by African-Americans and non–African-Americans, are inherently incapable of shedding perceptive light on the study of African-American cultural systems. Consequently, many interpretations of narrative events are not recognizable in the lives of the communities in which the research was conducted.

It is difficult to know the subtleties and complexities of any religious system. When that activity is as densely layered as preaching performances tend to be in African-American churches, conventional research approaches can be inadequate. As a result it was customary, until quite recently, to dismiss the affecting power of performed African-American folklore systems. Forms of African-American folklore were not assumed to be the result of complex series of judgments and organizing principles retrieved judiciously from cultural data banks as a conscious and manipulated process. The performance of African-American folklore, by African-Americans, is not generally regarded as rationalized acts seated in fully reasoning philosophical sensibilities. In a more general sense, the argument that holds a brief for the meta-folkloric capability of folk communities is still being waged uphill. But in few areas of research is this more clearly observable than in views on the African-American sermon.

In 1856, James Watson reported, "Two impressions rested vividly upon our mind: that among a people unlettered and ignorant, the highly emotional in religion is just as indispensable for the purposes of conversion as is the more intellectual among the educated and refined." In the same volume Watson reports on a sermon preached by Brother Carper, an African-American preacher, from which the following was excerpted:

> Dare be two kinds ob language, de literal and de figerative. De one expresses de tought plainly, but not passionately; de oder passionately, but not always so plainly. . . . De text [*Isaiah* 32:2] is an ensample of dat lubly stile of speech de figerative. ". . . and a man shall be as a hiding-place from the wind, and a covert from the tempest; as rivers of water in a dry land, as the shadows of a great rock in a wary land."[45]

While the Carper excerpt is not as elaborate a thesis as might be common in some sermons—assuming the transliteration is more or less faithful—it evidences the existence in African-American preaching of a canon on preaching. Carper sets forth rhetorical principles that serve as norms for the preacher, and he is certainly aware of differentiated speech functions and purposes in sermon discourse. In addition to the emotion that attends the African-American sermon in performance, there are instantaneously realized aesthetic dimensions and event-organizing principles levied during a sermon performance.

Rosenberg's charge of neglect of the African-American and American folk sermon is observable in the literature. It is apparent as well that scholars who have reported on the African-American sermon have suffered the influence of a set of powerful and related ideas: (1) emotionalism in pulpit performance and the inability to construct philosophic structures for performance systems are functions of illiteracy; (2) as communities gain education and literacy, folk forms will disappear. The pervasive presence of these notions in studies of African-American performance systems is alarming enough. But voluntary adherence to these ideas by researchers, in some cases in the face of lifelong experiences, indicts any scholarly enterprise that requires scholars to be obedient to perspectives that are not matched by the lives of scholar-hosting groups and communities.

A Definition of the African-American Sermon

Sermons, like any cultural form, adhere to "rules" of performance. Consequently, though such concepts as "formula" and "system" lend an inappropriate mechanical aura to a fundamentally creative, artistic form, when the high degree of oral formula and structure exhibited in African-American sermons is explored, the terms, used judiciously, are applicable and descriptive.

Central to any attempt to analyze folklore systems is the assumption that the analytic purpose is, as Hymes observes, "more than the placing of data in an articulated set of categories."[46] Still, many social scientists concerned with oral performance and oral phenomena interacting with the particulars of a culture, view structural analysis as inimical. And with the current interest displayed by many scholars in the structural analysis of folklore systems, there is certainly the possibility of limited creativity on the part of the analyst and a resultant misrepresentation of the form.

Hymes points out that "structural analysis [is] more than the placing of data in an articulated set of categories. Such placing is a necessary starting point, and also a desired outcome when systems that have been individually analyzed are studied comparatively. But for the individual systems, structural analysis means a scientific and moral commitment to the inductive discovery of units, criteria and patternings that are valid in terms of the system itself." Alan Dundes offers much the same response in his introduction to Vladimir Propp's *Morphology of the Folktale*, arguing, "clearly structural analysis is not an end in it-self! . . . It is a powerful technique of descriptive ethnography in-asmuch as it lays bare the essential form of the folkloristic text. But the form must ultimately be related to the culture or cultures in which it is found." Additionally, the new paradigms identified as a result of analy-sis will point to wider networks within the culture, some of which may not be explicitly related to expressive language functions, though they may depend upon the several functions of language to facilitate cogni-tion by culture participants. [47]

Many of the terms used in this study are found commonly in the folkloric, anthropological, and linguistic literatures. Without apology, the terms are reconceptualized here:

> *Formulaic*:   Milman Parry, whose work Albert Lord completed, defined "formulaic" as "a group of words regularly employed under the same metrical conditions to express a given idea." [48] The essential element in the Parry definition is the unit concept of meter. In this discussion the meter concept is shifted from its accustomed literary environment to a quasi-musicological en-vironment in which qualitative units of tempo and tone con-tours are more applicable. The reference frame is not a visual to mental process as in "visualizing" a poem, but rather a socio-auditory to sociopsychological to socio-oral environmental pro-cess, as in imploding a feeling and fashioning an appropriate, culturally sanctioned verbal response or gesture. While this concept is illustrated further on in this study, perhaps com-ments by Walter Ong will serve to draw attention to the multi-phenomenological character of the African-American sermon: "The world of a dominantly oral . . . culture . . . is dynamic . . . an event world rather than an object world. The voice is for man the paradigm of all sound, and to it all sound tends to be assimilated. The dynamism inherent in all sound tends to be as-similated to the dynamism of the human being. . . . The larger conceptual and verbal structures in which oral-aural man stores what he knows consists in great part of stories that turn on human action and on the interaction of man and man." [49] "Formulaic," then, can include formed sound groups and word groups that when taken together identify a narrative idea.
>
> *Theme*:   Lord defines "theme" as a "commonly used incident, de-scription, or idea which, regardless of content, uses many of the same formulas in approximately the same sequence." [50] My use of "theme" is a bit more conventional than Lord's and includes

subformula statements identifying the topic of a sermon, in addition to Lord's units.

Formulaic System: Lord's notion of "formulaic system" as a "verbal mold into which a variety of words are poured but which remains consistent through similarities of diction, syntax, accent and alliteration" is identified by Rosenberg as "patterns that make adjustment of phrase and creation of phrase by analogy possible." Rosenberg's visualization of a formulaic system is probably the most useful of these borrowed terms, but there are two basic elements that need to be isolated from the definition before proceeding. The use of syntax as a concept is critical here, for not only are word-phrase patterns being examined in the linguistic sense, but the arrangements of semantic secular codes in the sacred preaching environment must necessarily be considered as well. Rosenberg's notion of a verbal mold, perhaps borrowed from Propp, correctly represents the sermon as a fixed oral system with a determined number of open "slots" which can be filled with a limited number of narrative units per slot, with certain key formulas having a greater displacement range than others, providing for the overlapping of formulaic systems and sermon unity and continuity.

The foregoing, then, can be summarized as follows. An African-American sermon is a verbal mold readily recognized as such by African-Americans in performance; it usually has three or more units structured formulaically, is organized serially in performance, and is given cohesion through the use of thematic and formulaic phrases. Each part or unit of the verbal mold and the narrative system itself must be subordinated to a larger religious intent. The "larger intent" must embrace a concretized secular and an abstracted sacred polemic tension.

I am substantially concerned with revealing the nature of African-American sermonic style in such a way as to make possible the future comparison of several African-American narrative systems or genres. How the sermon is composed in performance is immensely important, as Rosenberg suggests. If the African-American sermon is composed "spontaneously," however, then understanding the organizational characteristics of the sermon genre, which presumes that the preacher is constantly making choices and manipulating the categories into which the material must be fitted for a "successful" sermon, becomes critical. The recognition of the organizing principles which support the sermon in performance is the key to the fruitful investigation of narrative creativity among African-Americans. Jokes, tales, political speeches, raps, toasts—all assume the form, if not the identical structure, of the African-American sermon when they are performed. Understanding the dynamics of the strong similarity in the performance of these genres which seem radically dissimilar lies in examining the African-American sermon and the environment in which the sermon is performed.[51]

Elder E. E. Cleveland at dedication of new Ephesians Church of
God in Christ, December 17, 1967.

E. E. Cleveland as evangelist at approximately age thirty-six.

Evangelist E. E. Cleveland with Cadillac touring car and driver.

Bishop E. E. Cleveland with a member of his congregation during Sunday services, February 1980.

Ephesians Church of God in Christ congregation gathering at altar for benediction and Circle of Fellowship, February 1980.

Ephesians Church of God in Christ congregation during the collection of
the offering, February 1980.

Evangelist E. E. Cleveland with sister and fellow evangelist
Maggie Cleveland, and accompanist (standing) Mrs. Iola Parker Jackson.
The trio was known as The Globetrotters.

Young women preparing to be baptized by Evangelist
E. E. Cleveland, Los Angeles.

Chapter Two

Oral Formula and the Performed African-American Sermon

Scholars who work with oral formula in folk narrative materials are appreciative of Lord's seminal study of oral epic composition technique and repertoire among Yugoslav guslars.[1] There is concern, however, that the predominance of Parry-Lord formulations in contemporary oral formula research, and the need to prove these formulations universally applicable to "spontaneous" folk narrative performance, has blunted the continuing development of oral formula theory. Donald Fry represents this concern as articulately as most:

> Scholars felt excessive reverence for Milman Parry's definition of the formula and waited too long to discard it. "A group of words which is regularly employed under the same metrical conditions to express a given essential idea" fits Homeric verse very well, but needs considerable modification to describe Old English techniques, which generates formulas from systems without any notion of an "essential idea."[2]

As Fry suggests, the popularity of the Parry-Lord formulations is out of proportion to the ability of these formulations to generate new thought in oral formula research. Parry's definition of formula is useful in setting an approach to the description of bodies of orally performed narratives, including the African-American sermon, but it is as problematical for me as it is for Frye.

Parry's primary morphologic unit, "a group of words which is regularly employed under the same metrical conditions to express a given essential idea," is not applicable to the African-American sermon. The principal morphologic unit of the African-American sermon is a *group of hemistich phrases shaped into an irrhythmic metrical unit when performed.* Since Parry's unit concept also includes the condition that the group of words should be "regularly employed under the same metrical conditions to express a given essential idea," it would appear that the two primary units share a fundamental similarity. However, the essential element in the Parry concept is the notion of meter, or regularly employed metrical patterns in oral performance. The essential elements in the primary African-American sermon unit are performed phrases of irregular length stretched or shortened to fit an oftentimes irrhythmic semantic sensibility. That is, in the African-American sermon, groups of phrases tend to have a seeming uniform metrical sense when performed, even though the lengths of sermon lines within a formula will vary widely.

The distinction is a crucial one. In his study of the African-American preacher, Rosenberg, inspired by Parry-Lord, arrived at the following conclusion on the nature of meter in the preacher's performance: "the oral preacher subordinates everything he has to say to the demands of his meter."[3] To illustrate the point, Rosenberg offers the following:

> Rev. Hays of Virginia was preaching the 116th Psalm when he erred and said the Psalmist was David. He corrected himself right away without breaking his meter or changing his timing. That such a change was planned or the language memorized seems extremely remote:
>
> David
> I gotta move on
> As he uttered these words
> He lay upon a sick bed
> Oh I don't mean David I mean
> The Psalmist
> If I won't make it correct me
> The Bible didn't say it was David
> When I get on the Psalms I almost
> Go right on—carrying on about David.[4]

Rosenberg's obvious concern is to make a statement on the "spontaneity" of African-American preaching. For Rosenberg, Parry and Lord offered a handle. But by extending the Parry-Lord formulation to the structure of the African-American sermon, Rosenberg "erred" in reading the event described above. In the illustration above, the Reverend Mr. Hays is more concerned with the accuracy of his spoken word than he is with the accuracy of his meter. Hay's meter was likely established earlier in the sermon. In order to make his correction, it was necessary for him to utilize the verbal pattern structure of the preceding line, to substitute one line for the other. The following admittedly crude notational representation of the Hays fragment under consideration might make the point clearer:

Oh I don't mean David I mean

The Psalmist

If I won't make it correct me

What is obvious by this illustration is that the Reverend Mr. Hays utilized the verbal pattern in the preceding line to generate "If I won't make it correct me." The pattern in the preceding line is in fact a mnemonic mechanism, helping Hays maintain his preaching fluidity and style.[5]

In sermon performance, the African-American preacher is principally concerned with the organization and the language of his sermon. The notion of meter in the sense of a rhythmic, mnemonic environment for the logical, pragmatic development of ideas, is not subordinate to the language focus. Rather, it is concurrent with it. The generation of structures for language usage and the structuring of rhythmic environments for the preacher's message are complementary, concurrent processes in the performance of African-American sermons.

This dual generative process is observable in several groups of lines, or sets, in Bishop Cleveland's sermon "He Wants Your Life: The Search for the Religion of Christ." In lines 3–5, Cleveland preaches:

3   Thank God for another opportunity to be home again
    Thank God for another opportunity to be here to bring you
        another message from the Lord
5   Thank God for the opportunity to preach on the search for the
        religion of Christ

In lines 20–24, the concurrent generating of language and eurhythmic structures is less marked than in the preceding example, but it is nonetheless observable:

20   Filled with anger and hate
     And filled with lust and pride and greed
     Filled with haughtiness and covetness
     Filled with doubts and fears
24   Why? Because they missed the mark

The concurrent generative process is more readily apparent in the following sets:

35   God is studying your tongue
     God is studying your aspirations
     God ain't studying your manipulations
     God ain't studying your demonstrations

       God ain't studying your words and your wisdom
40   God don't want your delay
41   God wants your life

70   And He wants your life
       He wants your motive
       He wants your intention
       He wants your purpose
74   He wants your objective
75   Say it with your life

96   Churches everywhere
       Churches in the basements
       Churches on the street corner
99   Churches in the storefronts and in the garages
       Churches in the dwelling house and
       Churches in the synagogues
       Churches everywhere
       Churches on the air twenty-four hours a day
104   Turn on the air and you'll hear somebody preaching church

206   And He wants lives
       He wants lives that will obey
       He wants lives that will be dedicated
       He wants lives to be consecrated
210   He wants lives to be sacrificed

For each of these formula sets, the lines immediately preceding
the sets do not seem to signal the imminent use of Cleveland's rhetorical enumerative technique:

1   Everybody say Amen
       Everybody say Amen

17   People can't sleep and rest
       Troubled and confused and perplexed
       Torn aggravated and agitated

33   Say it
       With your life

68   "Why call ye Me Lord and Master
       And won't do the thing I tell you?"

94   The world knows it and the church knows it
       More folk going to church now than ever in the history of the
          world

204 Jesus say, "He give Me more than all of you."
205 Thank God

In most of the sets, however, the generated formula is developed from a key word, idea, or phrase in the lines immediately preceding the set. In fact, of the six sets cited from the sermon text, five are in syntactic harmony with the immediately preceding lines. Only in the sixth set is there an apparent disjuncture with the immediately preceding line.

In lines 94 through 104, it is possible to observe Cleveland's expressive language generation system at work. In line 94, "church" shares subject status with "world." That is, both "church" and "world" are aware of the hypocrisy of those who are not as energetic about their faith in Christ as they are in secular pursuits. Seeming to have made a decision to use "church" as the key phrase in his next formula, Cleveland has to develop a transition mechanism between his first mention of church and its use in his generating formula. Line 96 serves that purpose. Cleveland inverts "church" and "world," moving church to the primary subjectival position and reducing "world" to secondary adjectival status. By so doing, Cleveland is now free to use "church" as the subject of the formula.

Cleveland's first phrase—"Churches everywhere"—opens the formula set. In the next five lines, churches are identified in a series of uncommon environments—basements, street corners, storefronts, homes, and synagogues. Churches are, indeed, everywhere. Cleveland's line 96 also serves as the initial rhythmical statement. That is, Cleveland articulates his base line for the set, all others will be patterned on it.

However, by the time Cleveland reaches line 102, he has decided to terminate this particular formula set, though it is not clear that he has decided where he wants to go. Line 99 is a *search phrase*, a line designated to expand the options for the generation of the next sermon unit. By line 104, Cleveland has seemingly decided to use "air," or the radio, and he has reduced "church" to adjectival status. (In fact, Cleveland mistakenly said "preaching" instead of "air.")

This important translation of message intent to language structure and mnemonic, rhythmic structures can be charted. For the African-American preacher the structuring of his words into useful rhythmic phrases is his most compelling concern. The Parry-Lord definition of formula that Rosenberg repeats in his examination of the African-American sermon is simply too narrow, too confining, to embrace the concurrent generating processes of language and eurhythmic structures

that attend the deployment of formula systems in African-American sermon performance.

Similarly, Lord's definition of theme as a "commonly used incident, description, or idea which, regardless of content, uses many
of the same formulas in approximately the same sequence" is not en-
compassing enough to include the African-American sermon.[6] And
Rosenberg dismisses the utilization of such a definition in the analysis
of the African-American sermon altogether! "Unlike epic narratives
whose themes are often necessary to the structure of the story," writes
Rosenberg, "the themes of the sermon are seldom necessary."[7] Rosenberg is mistaken. Themes are both necessary and fundamental to the
structures of the sermon in performance. The problem may be that the
definition of theme that arises from a close reading of the structures of
the African-American sermon are not as fanciful as Lord's because what
needs to be described is fairly straightforward. In African-American
sermon performance, theme is simply the stated, or strongly implied,
subject of the sermon. The preacher usually announces what he considers to be his theme from the pulpit as part of the text of the sermon.

In line 5 of Cleveland's sermon, he preaches:

5   Thank God for the opportunity to preach on the search for the
     religion of Christ

The theme here is obvious, Cleveland intends to take as his subject the
search for the religion of Christ. In Cleveland's key sermon, discussed
in chapter 1, however, the theme is slightly more difficult to identify,
although his congregation had little trouble recognizing it when it was
announced. He begins,

3   As I was coming up the street to church tonight
     Prayed as I walked along
5   The Lord gave me this message
7   But I wish you'd listen

Cleveland then read the fifty-ninth chapter of the Book of Isaiah.
Cleveland has not to this point announced his theme; Cleveland's congregation interprets Cleveland's use of the conjunctive "But" in line 7
to mean that the theme will be announced shortly. In fact, Cleveland
announces his theme in line 32:

28   And you know what the Lord said?
     I want you to repeat after me
30   The fault
     Is not in the Lord
32   You are just not ready

Through his use of pause and intonation, Cleveland makes it clear that line 32 is the awaited subject statement. The congregation seemed to delight in the delayed announcement. When questioned in an interview, one member of the congregation stated, with considerable enthusiasm, that this device was evidence of Cleveland's virtuosity. A more dispassionate reading is that Cleveland simply did not "discover" the title of the sermon until shortly before his announcement. The theme, however, was clear.

The Reverend Dr. Anderson is more consistently explicit than Bishop Cleveland. In the first sermon under consideration, Anderson states,

14   My theme is
15   In Times Like These

Again, in the second sermon, Anderson's theme statement is straightforward,

16   I want to use as my theme tonight
17   Ezekiel and the Vision of Dry Bones

The purpose of this discussion is not to draw comparisons between Bishop Cleveland and the Reverend Dr. Anderson. Rather it is to document that the announcement of theme is an obligatory part of the performed African-American sermon structure. Although this statement of theme is expected during the introductory sermon formula, it may be delayed until the second or third formulaic unit, but the statement must be made.

Rosenberg, however, is raising a more basic consideration than whether or not themes are identified by African-American preachers during the course of a sermon performance. Rosenberg's concern is whether or not the stated themes have a functional, structural capability within the sermon performance. It is one thing to state confidently that thematically related ideas, descriptions, or narrative genre—exempla, jokes, tales—are used in the sermon system to support and elucidate the sermon theme. It is quite another matter to produce the narrative environment in which the structural characteristics of theme and theme-related narrative events can be made comprehensible. And yet that is the nature of Rosenberg's challenge.

This narrative environment, the integrating context for formula, meter, and theme in the African-American sermon, is the *formulaic system*. Rosenberg's version of the formulaic system is the Propp-inspired "verbal mold" into which "a variety of words are poured but which remains consistent through similarities of diction, syntax, ac-

cent and alliteration," a definition which might have better served
Rosenberg in his discussion of meter.[8] The notion of the verbal mold is
especially useful as a rationalizing concept for the production of thematic formulas. It does not, however, identify the componential character of the African-American sermon. It is not the linking together of
analogous phrases that gives the African-American sermon its distinctive character. It is the utilization of independent narrative units held
together through the use of theme-related bridges. In this discussion
the thematic bridge mechanism is a category of formula that has
the specialized function of bridging the sermon's independent units
through restatements of the sermon's theme and by providing tempo-
rary closure for the preceding formula and entry into the next formula.

In the key sermon in this study—Bishop Cleveland's "You're Just
Not Ready"—formula, theme, and bridge are readily identifiable.
Cleveland's theme is preparation for entry into the Kingdom of God.
There are four major formulaic units in the Cleveland sermon. Each
unit has its own function in terms of amplifying an aspect of the theme
and advancing Cleveland's explanation and examination of the theme.
Additionally, each formulaic unit manifests the required sacred/secular
polarity, or tension, and each formulaic unit can be considered as having an "independent" existence within the environment of the performed sermon.

Formulaic unit number one is useful for illustrating the formula-
to-theme relationship:

   1 God bless you
       Everybody say Amen
       As I was coming up the street to church tonight
       Prayed as I walked along
   5 The Lord gave me this message
       And I didn't know what the choir was going to sing tonight
       But I wish you'd listen
       Isaiah, the fifty-ninth chapter said
       "Behold,
  10 The Lord's hands are not shortened
       That He cannot save
       Neither His ear heavy
       That He cannot hear
       But your iniquity has separated
  15 Between you and your God
       And your sins have hid His face from you
       That He will not hear
       For your hands are defiled with blood

Your fingers with iniquity
20   Your lips have spoken lies
Your tongue have muttered perverseness
None call for justice
Nor any plead for truth
They trust in vanity
25   And speak lies
They conceive mischief
And bring forth iniquity."
And you know what the Lord said?
I want you to repeat after me
30   The fault
Is not in the Lord
You are just not ready
God said here in Isaiah, the fifty-ninth chapter
The fault ain't in Me
35   I know you're just about to turn atheist
You're just about to say there ain't no God
You're just about to say I'm dead
But the fault ain't in Me
You're just not ready
40   For My blessings
Hallelujah to God
Your iniquity have separated between you and your God
And your sins have hid His face from you
You speak lies and perverse things
45   Thank God
And it's because of you that you can't get the blessing
It doesn't mean that you can't get married now
Plenty folks get married
But everybody ain't ready to get married
50   You haven't got your blood test
You haven't got your license
You haven't got your divorce
It's not final
You got six more months to go
55   So you are not ready
To get married
And folks are getting married every day
Glory to God
It don't mean that there are not jobs
60   There are plenty jobs
You go in there and apply for a job

They throw a question or a sheet
In your face
Answer these questions
65   And if you can't answer them
You're just not ready
The job is for the fella that can fill out the application
And answer this question
Plenty colleges and you can get scholarships
70   But everybody can't go to college
'Cause you're just not ready
They go back and pick up that record where you made "B's" and
   "C's" and "D's"
My God
How many time you ducked school
75   You're just not ready
And they got counselors there at school
To keep you from being so disappointed
And come out such a frizzled mess
They say
80   Listen, you go before the counselor
And let him tell you whether or not you ready for college
Let him tell you whether or not you ready to study to be a doctor
   or a lawyer
He'll get your records and say
No, you're just not ready
85   Say, you take home economics
You take agriculture
You go take social work
Go to asking folks how long they been on the welfare
You are not ready
90   For Me to answer your questions
You are not ready
God said
You just not ready
For Me to give you your request
95   If you get ready
Man, in quicker than the flash of an eye
I'll come while you call
While you just preachin'
I'll answer
100   My God
Get ready

> You'll have to go with Me
> If you just decide
> I'll give you the size of your heart
105 But you got to be ready
> Oh, praise God
107 Hallelujah

The African-American sermon formula was earlier identified as the primary morphological unit of the genre and was defined as "a group of hemistich phrases shaped into irrhythmic metric units when performed to express an integral element in the development of the sermon's theme." The "integral element in the development of the sermon's theme" expressed in this first of Cleveland's formulaic units in the key sermon is a general commentary on the need to be prepared for any of life's involvements. The "need to be prepared" is initially expressed in the general terms, in the sacred context, of preparing oneself to receive God's blessing (lines 33–44). Cleveland next moves to a series of secular contexts in which the "preparedness" principle is applied to marriage, applying for a job, applying for college admission (lines 45 to 89). Finally, Cleveland returns to the generalized sacred context for the formula summation: if one is prepared for an engagement, then success is swift and immediate (lines 90 to 105). The preparedness principle is reinterpreted in each of the sermon's three remaining formulaic units with increasing specificity.

Coincidentally, the theme statement, "You are just not ready," is both a free clause formula having the range of the entire sermon and a bridge.[9] In addition to serving a transition function between formulaic units (line 105) and subformulaic segments (lines 32 and 89), the "You are just not ready" bridge is used at several points in the formulaic unit for rhetorical effect, to heighten the drama, the theater of the preaching (lines 39, 66, 71, 75, 84). When used in this manner, the bridge has the effect of litany and intensifies both the theme and the application of the theme.

The phrases that shape each sermonic unit are not regular. They are, in fact, hemistich or irregular in length. They are made metrically "regular"—given a sense of patterned consistency—in the performance of the sermon, and always in the environment of other hemistich phrases. It is oftentimes difficult to discern any regular metrical value from the scansion of a single phrase or line. Line 99 in the key sermon, "I'll answer," has neither pattern sense nor value by itself. Only when evaluated in the context of other, related phrases does the phrase achieve meaning.

98 While you just preachin'
99 I'll answer
    My God
    Get ready
    You'll have to go with Me
    If you just decide
104 I'll give you the size of your heart
    But you got to be ready

Obviously it is necessary to evaluate an entire sermon narrative unit—
a formulaic unit or a subformula unit—to discover a useful, integral
patterned sensibility. The Parry definition of formula that insists on
consistent metric units is simply not applicable. It is imprecise and
ambiguous in the African-American preaching context. The African-
American preacher is not concerned with phrase-by-phrase metrical
consistency, although rhythm serves a mnemonic function. He is concerned with a phrasing pattern that serves his semantic purpose and
his sensibility, his rhetorical style.

The use of larger-than-phrase units in this analysis makes possible
the discovery of another unique feature of the African-American sermon structure. In the preaching of the sermon, each formula must embrace specifically identifiable secular references from daily or "street"
life and abstracted or generalized sacred references from the Scriptures or application of the Scriptures. In formula number one of the
key sermon, the polarity is apparent. Lines 1 through 46 of the formula
are entirely taken up with the reading of a chapter of the Bible to support Cleveland's theme, and a Scripture-based pedagogy. Lines 47
through 88 constitute the secular hemiparadigm of the formula and
are filled with specific, concrete references from the secular lives of
African-Americans. Lines 89 through 107 complete the formula and return the congregation to the secular environment.

The sacred and secular units of the formula maintain a distinct
character in the sermon. Theme-related phrases of varying lengths—
sacred hemiformulas/irregular meter; secular hemiformula/regular
meter—as well as role assumption by the preacher are devices used to
signal onset and decay in the development of formulaic units. The
preacher, through a change in meter or other devices, will alert the
congregation to an imminent shift in the polarities.

The foregoing, then, can be summarized as follows: an African-
American sermon is a performed verbal mold based in one stated
theme, developed through four or more independent subthematic for-

mulaic units unified by thematic bridges, or free-clause formulas. Each component of the verbal mold and the verbal mold itself must be subordinated to a larger concern for a concretized secular and an abstracted sacred balance.

THE "WEIGHTED SECULAR" FACTOR
IN THE PERFORMED AFRICAN-AMERICAN SERMON

To those who regularly and attentively listen to African-American sermons performed by African-American preachers, the similarities in varied preaching circumstances are striking. An African-American sermon preached in Oakland, California, will sound similar to an African-American sermon preached in Boston, Massachusetts. The African-American sermon, as with folk narrative materials generally, is developed within a rigid framework of rules and custom. In the case of the sermon materials, that framework is in part traditional and historical, which in large measure accounts for the perceived similarity in African-American sermon performance.

In *Black Preaching* Henry Mitchell, an African-American theologian and preacher, notes some of the characteristics of African-American sermon performance that he considers to be the "rules" of the genre. More precisely, Mitchell articulates a canon on African-American pulpit performance.

> The Black fathers (preachers) knew and followed . . . rules long before the Teutons spelled out the new hermeneutic. The first is that one must declare the gospel in the language and culture of the people—the vernacular. For some this involves resistance to a temptation to be learned and proper. To the Black fathers this was no problem . . . the best of Black preachers today still know intuitively that they have no allegiance to any cultural criteria save the idiom of the people. . . . there can be no wonder as to why the educated contemporary Black preacher is not the least tempted to leave the Black style. . . . The second hermeneutic principle is that the gospel must speak to contemporary man and his needs. The Black fathers felt no compulsion to be orthodox or accepted. . . . On the contrary, they look for the answer to Black people's needs.[10]

The significance of Mitchell's observation is apparent. In order to be most effective and efficient, the African-American sermon is preached in the language of the congregation, including idiomatic and other colloquial forms. So efficient is sermonic style and structure among African-Americans that politicians and "good talkers" generally have adopted the form and adapted it to secular purposes. Still, it is the African-American preacher who continues to employ the genre in the form most recognizable to African-American people.

By mentioning that "the gospel must speak to the contemporary man and his needs [and] . . . Black fathers . . . look for the answer to Black people's needs," Mitchell enters the debate on the presumed "other worldly" character of African-American sermon themes.[11] The definition of an African-American sermon demands recognition of a sacred/secular tension or polarity in the structure of the performed sermon. On this point, Mitchel and I are in agreement. The generalized sacred elements of a sermon formulaic unit must always appear in the same morphological environment with specifically referenced secular elements. So careful is the preacher to include specific, contemporary secular elements in his sermon formulas that the structuring of this element in the preaching seems to claim a greater portion of the preacher's creative energies. In contrast, sacred referencing seems to be casual and is obviously the result of a reasonably stable body of knowledge. This concentration on the secular reference can be considered the "weighted secular factor" in African-American preaching. The demonstrated presence of this factor, and the process which generates it, in the sermons of African-American preachers argues convincingly for the point Mitchell offers: the African-American preacher's principal mission is to speak to the contemporary needs of his congregation.

A historical dimension on this point was provided by the non–African-American Rev. James Watson in 1856 in his *Tales and Takings*. Watson noted in his description of Brother Carper's sermon that the sermon began with a Bible reading, Isaiah 32:2:

> "And a man shall be as a hiding-place from the wind, and a covert from the tempest; as rivers of water in a dry place, as the shadow of a great rock in a weary land."[12]

In a series of formulas, Brother Carper goes on to explore each phrase of the Bible text, paying careful attention to topographical description. Near the end of the sermon, the intent of the topographic detail seems to come clear. Brother Carper appears to be describing, figuratively if not literally, an escape route, which Watson dismisses as naive ramblings.

> A shout ob danger from de more resolute captain ob de caravan am sent along de ranks, prolonged by a thousand thirst-blistered tongues, commingled in one ceaseless howl ob woe, varied by ebery tone ob distress and despair. To "de great rock," shouts de leader as 'pon his Arab hoss he heads dis flight to de Refuge. . . . before dem, in de distance, a

mighty great rock spreads out its broad and all-resisting sides, lifting its
narrowing pint 'bove the clouds, tipped wid de sun's fiery blace, which
had burnt 'pon it since infant creation 'woke from de cradle ob kaos at
de call of its Fader.
   (Here our sable orator pointed away to some of the spurs of the
Ozark Mountains seen off to the northwest through a forest opening, at
a distance of from ten to fifteen miles, and whose summits of barren
granite blazed in the strength of a clear June sun, like sheeted domes on
distant cathedrals.)
   Dat light de be light ob hope, and dat rock be do rock ob hope to
de now flyin' weepin' faintin' and famishin' hundred. De captain has arrived dare.
   (Here a suppressed cry of "Thank God," escaped many of the
audience.)[13]

Reminding his congregation once again that he is using "figera-
tive," or symbolic, language, Brother Carper refers to his opening
Bible text in the conclusion of his sermon:

See, he has disappeared behind it, perhaps to explore its cavern coverts.
But see, he has soon re-appeared and wid joy dancing in his eye, he
stands shoutin' and beckonin', "Onward, onward, onward, ONWARD,"
when he reels from weariness and falls in behind the rock. ("Thank
God, he's saved!" exclaimed a voice.)[14]

However fanciful the interpretation of this sermon might appear,
it is clear that it has an extraordinarily high political purpose. The
preacher, Brother Carper, skillfully and artfully bends the churchly
sermonic form to an expressly political end, the spiritual and physical
liberation of African-Americans. In each sermon formula, Carper bal-
ances biblical reference against topographic fact relevant to the region
in which the congregation is located. The whole sermon, indeed the
church service, is pushed toward one goal, liberation in the secular
environment.
   In the preceding section of this chapter, a similar identification of
the weighted secular and nonspecific sacred factors in the African-
American sermon formula was made in a formula of Bishop Cleveland's
key sermon. Those factors are commonplace in the sermon formulas of
African-American preachers.
   It is not my purpose to argue that the African-American preacher
and the African-American performed sermon are in the vanguard of political liberation movements in the United States. Unfortunately, the
African-American preacher has far too frequently represented and
identified with nonprogressive social and political units in American
communities, particularly when the preacher has moved from pulpit to

secular platform. E. Franklin Frazier even suggests that the Black preacher has helped the African-American "to become accommodated to an inferior status."[15] The point remains, however, that whatever the political views and sentiments of the African-American preacher, he is intimately attuned to the daily secular needs of his congregation and to the social and political environment in which Black life in the United States is lived and acted out. He may use the perfection of the Christian life as example, as framework, but his focus is riveted on his congregation's need to live a fully experiencing daily, secular existence. Hence, the "weighted secular" factor in African-American sermon performance is a key concept in distinguishing the African-American sermon from the sermons of other cultural groups.

Chapter Three

Characteristics and Functions of the Structural Units of the African-American Sermon

An African-American sermon has been defined as "a performed verbal mold based on one stated theme, developed by the utilization of four or more independent narrative formulaic units, with pairs or groupings of formulaic units unified by theme-related independent or free clauses.[1] Each component of the verbal mold (the performed African-American sermon), and the verbal mold itself, is subordinated to a larger concern for a concretized secular and abstracted sacred balance." "Performed verbal mold" is synonymous with genre; "stated theme" is the preacher's announced subject.

The conceptualization of "independent subthematic formulaic units" is more problematical than either "performed verbal mold" or "stated theme." There is a seeming contradiction in the notion of an "independent" narrative unit that would seem to derive a substantial part of its integrity from a dependent relationship to other parts of the narrative system. It would seem that if a unit can be considered independent, then all of the qualities required to prescribe the unit are present within the unit. A brick, for instance, does not receive its primary definitive characteristics in the environment of a building; it has a unique character, a "presence," in its own right.

A peculiarity of the African-American sermon formulaic unit is that by its very nature it is capable of an existence apart from the sermon. Indeed, the appearance of a formulaic unit in the sermon may be directly related to the strength of the formula as a narrative event in a secular environment. In the Reverend Dr. Anderson's "In Times Like These," he preaches the following:

94 These are times when many are turning back into the world of sin
95 Oh, the countless Christians that are going back into the
   wilderness
   Some are fading, and some are doubting

These are times of spiritual darkness
Of moral weakness
100   With millions of church members on the fence of indecision
101   *Trying to run with the hare and 'ho with the hound* [emphasis
          added]

In general use in American folklore and literature, the rabbit frequently
is recognized for his fecundity, while among African-Americans "hound"
is used to describe the alleged free-wheeling sexuality of African-
American men ("hound" meaning "cockhound").[2] To "'ho with the
hound" means joining buddies in carousing with women (to go whoring
with the hound).

But the metaphoric sexuality of the line is misleading. Anderson is
not suggesting that church members are unwilling to make a commitment to Christianity because they are wallowing in libertine and dis-
solute sexuality. His message is considerably more existential. He is
calling for the sort of balanced tensions between secular experience
and sacred application in one's African-American existence that is reflected in the worldview structure of the performed African-American
sermon. The abstracted sacred and concrete secular aspects of the
African-American sermon discussed earlier do not represent, and are
not intended to represent, a model moral existence. These bipolarities
do not constitute an inviolable prescribed pattern for a Christian life
for African-Americans. Rather, they are representative of an ideal political, social, and cultural existence for African-Americans. Anderson's
point is made in the context of the perverse turmoil of American social
politics, and the disproportionate commitment many of his congregation have made to purely secular hedonistic pursuits.

This consideration speaks directly to those scholars who argue
that African-American preaching is limited to raising the emotions of
African-American congregations.[3] Many African-American preachers
can speak in "codes." The codes have a pragmatic function for congregations. They are the images of the sermon through which the congregation is invited to share in the artistry of the master storyteller, to
be carried by the preacher's vision. The preacher is the pastor of his
flock, and he artfully, deftly, guides his congregation through the rigors
and temptations of daily secular living. Both preacher and congregation share in the encoding and deciphering of sermon element. When
this complex, concurrent activity is most intense, the only suitable responses are sound or word-absent phrases—those "moans," "cries,"
and "shouts" so underestimated by Davis, Crowley, and Pipes and appreciated by Mitchell.[4]

Any structure has an integral support system, an infrastructure that is the product of design, intention, and historically developed rationalizations. Such a created event may likely have an exostructure as well, an external "surface" upon which the individuating genius of the creating faculty makes his creative statement. The external surface completes the intention of the crafting personality; it is the vehicle that permits the crafting mind to exhibit his or her personal sensibility. Therefore, any consideration of a "whole" structure must include an examination both of the internal characteristics that are generic to all examples of the type and of the surface of the structure in order to evaluate the nature of the intentional "performance."

The African-American sermon has an infrastructure. That is, the structural units of the sermon and the series of rationales and philosophic valuations that support a particular unit in a particular space can be thought of as the sermon's internal "system." The performed African-American sermon is a narrative system which incorporates rationalized sets of conventions and principles designed to support the articulation of existence, belief, and cosmologic considerations in the experiencing lives of African-American people. The African-American preacher verbally reconstructs his sermon infrastructure as he preaches, in accordance with the established, rationalized conventions and principles of the African-American sermon system.

Each unit of the sermon must be properly ordered, within the sermon structure, before the preacher can move on to the next formulaic unit. Obviously this is useful to the preacher for mnemonic purposes, and his knowledge of the sermon system allows him greater expressive and creative latitude in laying his personality over the sermon's infrastructure. In the course of performing a sermon, a preacher will progressively move away from mechanical adherence to the principles of infrastructure construction, although the infrastructure maintains a constant and recognizable presence in the sermon, toward elaboration and creative illustration of the sermon theme. The preacher will return to the recognizable infrastructure, however, by the end of the sermon.

This dynamic can be illustrated through a closer examination of those structural units that are utilized in the development of the sermon's infrastructure. In gross terms, these are the minimal requirements for the realization of an African-American sermon. While the preacher is expected to take creative liberties during the course of thematic elaboration and formula unit generation, he is bound by tradition to include several elements in his sermon performance.

A. The preacher informs his congregation that his sermon text is not his own, that he did not arbitrarily decide the text of his sermon. The African-American preacher must indicate to his congregation that the text of his sermon was provided by Divine intervention, by God. The following excerpts from the sermons of Bishop Cleveland and Rev. Dr. Anderson illustrate this point.

CLEVELAND SERMON NO. 1

3   As I was coming up the street to church tonight
    Prayed as I walked along
5   *The Lord gave me this message* [emphasis added]

CLEVELAND SERMON NO. 2

3   Thank God for another opportunity to be home again
    Thank God for another opportunity to be here *to bring you*
       another message from the Lord [emphasis added]

ANDERSON SERMON NO. 1

19   We have been blessed by the visitation of the Holy Spirit

ANDERSON SERMON NO. 2

21   And this is one message from the Lord that you cannot run
     away from it

The postponing of the obligatory mention of God's sanction until several lines following the identification of the announced theme seems to be an idiosyncrasy of the Reverend Dr. Anderson. In the first sermon, recognition follows theme identification by eight lines. In the second sermon, recognition of God's intercession in the discovery of the sermon text follows the announcement of the theme by five lines.

Invoking God's sanction in the performance of the sermon in African-American worship is consistent with the notion of the "call," the concept that one has been "chosen" by God to pursue a career in the ministry. Even though the ministry as a profession in which ministers are trained formally in universities is increasingly commonplace in African-American churches, ministers and preachers do frequently serve an apprenticeship under the stewardship of older pastors. Most conventional African-American churches require a preacher to show evidence that he has been "called" to preach. The "call" can be identified in any number of ways: through conversion; through a "sign," which may be interpreted by the church elders; through evidence of healing powers; by verification that a male was born with a cowl or veil over his head. It is generally acknowledged that the nature of a "call" is mysterious and requires special talents for verification.

A call to preach, however, is not to be confused with the preacher's ability to respond to frequent messages and signs from God and the interpretation of those signs or messages through his sermon theme. Although a preacher may not be required by his congregation to lead a fully exemplary life, he is expected to conduct his personal affairs in a manner which does not reflect adversely on his congregation and church. When the African-American preacher assumes his pulpit, he reaffirms for himself and his congregation his "chosen" role as God's messenger. He is the intermediary between God and the congregation.

Identifying God as the source for the message, at the beginning of the African-American sermon, is the equivalent of a tale's opening formula. It is a verbal show of respect and deference to the Creator while making clear the preacher's own privileged position with respect to God. It is a verbal libation of sorts. It is the convincing invocation of this patronage that permits the preacher to continue leading his flock.

His Grace, King Narciss, however, rarely accomplishes this first threshold. While it is assumed that Narciss is a man of God, he does not feel obligated to reaffirm his patronage when he steps into the pulpit to preach. But neither is he arrogant and presumptuous in his seeming disregard for the tradition of sermon development in African-American sermon performance. Rather, Narciss comes to the development of sermon units with a different set of generating principles. He is, in a fundamental sense, philosophically at odds with Cleveland and Anderson. For instance, Narciss preaches:

10   Each Sunday we talk to you
      Endeavoring to express God to you

He continues,

12   God in spirit
      And God in truth
      But because there are so many spirits here
15   And they're housed in various bodies
      Each spirit tries to make it's presentation
      They ask Jesus this question
18   "To whom should we give honor to?"

In effect, Narciss has significantly altered the customary three-tiered configuration that places the African-American preacher in the mediating position between God and the congregation. It is entirely possible that Narciss, the most eclectic of the three preachers discussed in this study, knowingly borrowed this philosophical stance from the Society of Friends (Quakers), whose literature is known to him.[5] This would not be unusual for Narciss's ministry, for in addition to the Lord's Prayer, he uses the Hail Mary, both chanted antiphonally, during the course of his sermon. The explanation offered by a follower was that the Hail Mary allowed Narciss to honor men and women, the Lord and His Mother. The Narciss configuration recognizes that the Spirit of God can descend on himself and his congregation concurrently but that he has a special obligation to instruct his congregation in the interpretation of God's visitation.

It is important to note that Narciss also recognizes and respects the impact Godly design can have on the selection of sermon themes, even though he does so far less than Cleveland or Anderson. Narciss finds it at least as valuable and necessary to reaffirm his own sensibilities from the pulpit as to use the more conventional opening employed by Cleveland and Anderson.

In summary, at the beginning of the African-American sermon, the preacher is obligated to demonstrate to his congregation that the authority for his sermon performance emanates from a guiding force beyond himself, in God, Christ, or more generally, the Creator.

B.   The next obligatory step in the development of the African-American sermon is the identification of the sermon's theme. Usually the identification of theme is followed by an appropriate, supporting Bible quotation, as in the following illustrations:

CLEVELAND SERMON NO. 1

    5   The Lord gave me this message
        And I didn't know what the choir was going to sing tonight
        But I wish you'd listen
        Isaiah the fifty-ninth chapter said
        "Behold,
   10   The Lord's hands are not shortened
        That He cannot save
        Neither His ear heavy
        That He cannot hear
        But your iniquity has separated
   15   Between you and your God
        And your sins have hid His face from you
        That He will not hear
        For your hands are defiled with blood
        Your fingers with iniquity
   20   Your lips have spoken lies
        Your tongue have muttered perverseness

None call for justice
Nor any plead for truth
They trust in vanity
25 And speak lies
They conceive mischief
And bring forth iniquity."
And you know what the Lord said?
I want you to repeat after me
30 The fault
Is not in the Lord
32 You are just not ready [sermon's theme]

CLEVELAND SERMON NO. 2

5 Thank God for the opportunity to preach on the search for
the religion of Christ
It's a blessed thing to be able to preach the Gospel in a time
like this
Men looking for something everywhere
The world is in search for something and it don't know what
they looking for
But we found it
10 And it's all in Jesus
He said without any doubt or disputation
"Come to Me
13 All ye that labor and are heavy laden and I'll give you rest."

ANDERSON SERMON NO. 1

3 You may turn with me to the sixth chapter of our Lord's
Gospel according to St. John and we're going to read the
5 Sixty-sixth to the sixty-ninth verses where you will find the
words of
The text. St. John's, chapter, six, verses sixty-six through sixty-
ninth
"From that time, many of His disciples went back and walked
no more
With Him. Then said Jesus unto the Twelve 'Will ye also go
away?'
Then Simon Peter answered Him, 'Lord to whom shall we
go?
10 Thou hast the words of eternal life and we believe and are
And are sure that Thou art that Christ, the Son of the Living
God.'"

I shall use as my theme tonight
Seeing the condition of the world
The people that is in it
15   My theme is
In times like these
17   In times like these

ANDERSON SERMON NO. 2

1   If you have your Bibles ready
You may turn with us
To the thirty-seventh chapter of the Book of Ezekiel
And we're going to read
5   The first, second and third verse
"The hand of the Lord
Was upon me
And carried me out in the Spirit of the Lord
And set me down
10   In the midst of the valley which was full of bones."
You understand that
"And cause me to pass by them round about
And behold there were very many in the open valley
And Lo, they were very dry."
15   You understand me
I want to use as my theme tonight
Ezekiel and the Vision of Dry Bones
You understand
Not dry bones in the valley
20   But Ezekiel and the Vision of Dry Bones

Narciss, who consistently modifies the conventional structures of the African-American sermon, identifies Bible verses early in the sermon. But unlike either Cleveland or Anderson, Narciss weaves the biblical quotations into the narrative of the performed sermon.

NARCISS SERMON

17   They ask Jesus this question
"To whom should we give honor to?"
But He being a spirit
20   He knew their craftiness
And from among them came a penny
And He asked them
"And whose inscription came upon this penny?"
And they said "Caesar"

25   And He said
"Give unto Caesar that which belongs to Caesar
And unto God, that which belongs to God"
28   I'm not satisfied with just my accomplishments alone

Narciss returns to the more conventional African-American sermon form and quotes a Bible verse that, seemingly, supports his as yet unannounced sermon theme.

33   He said unto them when they asked Him about the spirits
He said to them in the fifteenth chapter of St. John
35   "I am the true vine"

For the African-American preacher and his congregation, knowledge of the Bible and the ability to use Bible verses liberally and appropriately to apply to any phase of life are the hallmarks of the true follower of Christ. In much the same way Yoruba men are raised in environments in which facility in the development and application of proverbs frequently determines the level of resources of the community or family to be set aside for the use of the young man, for education for instance, African-American preachers and their congregations frequently engage in contests to see who can quote a Bible verse most applicable to a given situation.[6] It is not uncommon for older church members to drill youngsters in the acquisition and use of Bible-based stories, quotations, and interpretations.

By quoting a Bible verse in support of his announced theme, the preacher is "proving" to his congregation his continuing ability to respond spontaneously from the depth of his Christian commitment. A function of the Bible quotation is to intensify the nature of the Godly sanction that attends the sermon performance. Bishop Cleveland's statement that his message came to him on his way to church that particular morning; the Reverend Dr. Anderson's careful equation of the "visitation of the Lord" with a good sermon; an admission by His Grace, King Narciss that his message came to him just before the service as he listened to other services over the radio, all serve to illustrate to the various congregations that the preacher is truly a chosen messenger of the Lord.

The sense of spontaneity notwithstanding, there is ample evidence that many African-American preachers have given considerable thought to their sermon texts days before the sermon is performed. While the preparation may not be as elaborate as in writing a sermon, it is clear that a considerable amount of forethought has gone into the text and certain features of elaboration. For example, at the denominational annual conventions attended by preachers, the various church publishing houses make available theme and text guides the preacher may utilize in the preparation of his sermons. This is not to diminish the power or complexity of the oral construction of a sermon but rather to suggest that oftentimes the core ideas of a sermon and the dazzling use of obscure Bible quotations may be owing to a published guide. Frequently, as in the case of the Reverend Dr. Anderson's "In Times Like These" sermon, little time has been spent preparing the sermon and the result can be disastrous, a point to be considered later.

The African-American preacher is under a considerable amount of pressure from his congregation. He may preach three full services on a Sunday and conduct as many services during the week. It may very well be that the seeming stock nature of sermonic themes and biblical references owes to the need continually to appear spontaneous under such circumstances. In any event, the quotation of biblical verses and the announcement of related themes are important stages in the development of the African-American sermon in performance.

C.   The final phase of the obligatory introductory phases in the development of the sermon is also the threshold of the sermon formulaic systems. Following the Bible quotations, the preacher is obliged and expected to interpret, first literally then broadly, the quoted Bible passage.

CLEVELAND SERMON NO. 1

33   God said here in Isaiah, the fifty-ninth chapter
      The fault ain't in Me
35   I know you're just about to turn atheist
      You're just about to say there ain't no God
      You're just about to say I'm dead
      But the fault ain't in Me
      You're just not ready
40   For my blessings
      Hallelujah to God
      Your iniquity have separated between you and your God
      And your sins have hid His face from you
      You speak lies and perverse things
45   Thank God
      And it's because of you that you can't get the blessing
      [end of literal interpretation, beginning of broad
         interpretation]
      It doesn't mean that you can't get married now
      Plenty folks get married
49   But everybody ain't ready to get married

CLEVELAND SERMON NO. 2

12   "Come to Me
     All ye that labor and are heavy laden and I'll give you rest
     This old world is laboring
15   Laboring
     Laboring night and day
     People can't rest and sleep
     Troubled and confused and perplexed
19   Torn, aggravated and agitated

ANDERSON SERMON NO. 1

27   From the Scriptures read and others that will be quoted or
        read later
     We shall speak to you from the theme In Times Like These
     Children, when we think rightly about our past you know
30   We know that it is our assigned duty and our faithfullness is
     The performance of our assigned duty. But first we would
     Like to appraise our times
     Help me Lord Jesus
     What's wrong with our times?
35   What's good or bad in times like these?
     What's good children .
     Or what is bad?
38   These are times of great excitement

ANDERSON SERMON NO. 2

16   I want to use as my theme tonight
     Ezekiel and the Vision of Dry Bones
     You understand
     Not dry bones in the valley
20   But Ezekiel and the Vision of Dry Bones

29   Now this new Ezekiel signifies God's way of thinking
     Ezekiel is known as one of the most mysterious Hebrew
        prophets
     Yes sir
     And he began, well, as a boy
     He grew up under the influence of Jeremiah
     And he began to prophesy at the age of thirty
35   And for twenty-two years preached by the River of Shafar
     [Anderson catalogs aspects of Ezekiel's ministry and develops
        formulaic sequences around each aspect]

NARCISS SERMON

35   "I am the true vine"
     For they have heard about the vine
     They had heard about the Messiah
     Like unto you
     They had heard the enchantment of thousands of voices

While Rosenberg minimizes, Mitchell more accurately concep-
tualizes this particular juncture in the development of the sermon.
Rosenberg casually offers the following observation: "When a preacher
starts his sermon he very often reads from the Bible and gradually
breaks away from the printed word toward his own rhythm and meter;
in order to do so he has to tell the Bible story in his own language,
making such additions and deletions as he feels necessary to maintain
his meter."[7] Mitchell writes:

> Good storytelling . . . biblical or nonbiblical, requires a sense of tim-
> ing. The teller must give enough details and action to keep the story
> moving and compel attention. Yet, he must also measure his pace so
> that the story is understood and the hearer stays abreast of the action in
> his identification with the narrative. This is especially true in the Black
> sermon. . . . Black Bible stories are to be relived, not merely heard.
> This requires a certain expertise in timing and emphasis so that atten-
> tion is not distracted on the one hand by the effort to keep up or by
> boredom on the other.[8]

Although both Cleveland and Anderson identify their themes during
their interpretation of the quotation, it is clear that the quotation and
the interpretation are symbiotic functions in the development of the
sermon. Rosenberg is misleading in his comment on the casual nature
of the relationship between the Bible verse and its interpretation. That
relationship is anything but casual.

The functional purpose of this particular juncture is closer to the
purposes of storytelling Mitchell comments on. This unit is technically
a transition, not from the printed word to the chanted sermon proper,
but from the "cool" world of stated doctrine to the "hot" environment
of everyday application of doctrine to experience. The shift from the
reading of the verse to the interpretation is fairly rapid. It is a shift
from an antiemotional state to an environment in which the preacher's
voice and sound become mechanisms for action and reflection.

D.   The body of the African-American sermon is constructed of
     independent theme-related formulas. Each unit of the for-
     mula develops or retards a secular and sacred tension and

moves between abstract and concrete example. Each generated formula is an aspect of the "argument" of the announced theme and advances the discovery and examination of the sermon theme.

Previously, "formula" was defined as a "group of hemistich phrases shaped into an irrhythmic unit when spoken to express an aspect of a central theme." The irregularity of the sermonic line is made rhythmic, not uniformly rhythmical, through the techniques of melisma, dramatic pause, emphatic repetition, and a host of devices commonly associated with African-American music. The most important characteristic of the formula, however, is not the irrhythmic line. The most important characteristics of the African-American sermonic formula are the groups of irrhythmic lines shaped around a core idea. Metrical consistency is not an essential feature of the African-American sermon, although an apparent and deliberately measured affective oratorical style is required.

For the purpose of illustration, the following formula occurs in Anderson's first sermon, "In Times Like These."

34   What's wrong with our times?
35   What's good or bad in times like these?
     What's good children?
     Or what is bad?
     These are times of great excitement
     And I'm sure you'll agree with me
40   But did you know that out of all of this
     Happening around us
     There are many so-called Christians
     Who are yet asleep?
     Spiritually asleep?
45   My, my, my

This excerpt from Anderson's sermon meets the requirements of the African-American sermon narrative formulaic unit. The performed phrases are not of uniform length, and are therefore hemistich, and evidence a seeming metrical consistency when spoken by Anderson. (Even the widely known and reported "I Have A Dream" sermon preached by Martin Luther King, Jr., is *seemingly* uniformly metrical.[9]) The formula illustration, lines 34–45, is in fact comprised of two subformulas. The first subformula includes lines 34–37, the setting up of the syllogism, the posing of the problem. The second subformula includes lines 38–44 and offers a resolution, of sorts, to the questions raised in the preceding subformula. Line 45 is important because it completes the "sense" of the formula and because it has a stylistic function in terms of signaling closure for the formula. As a caveat, it would also be noted that the two subformulas manifest the sacred/secular "tension" or polarity earlier identified as obligatory in the African-American sermon. Lines 34–37 pose a general and abstract query, "in these historical times, what are the causes of man's problems?" The answer, which is less than convincing, is provided in specific terms in lines 38–44: "too many Christians have forgotten the obligations of their commitments." Line 45, "My, my, my" is Anderson's comment on the profundity of the syllogism, a signal that the formula has been concluded, and a recognized code used to indicate an imminent transition.

The twelve-line formula, as an introductory unit of Anderson's sermon, is a preface to a step-by-step examination of the announced theme. This formula sets the framework of the sermon's rhetorical infrastructure.

Since the sermon phrases are irregular, techniques that explain the ability of the preacher, like blues performers and rhythm and blues performers, to produce a phrasing structure that to the listener seems regular and consistent are worth noting. The technique that the preachers most frequently use is syllabic increase, sometimes known as "worrying" a line, or the elongation of a word through creative syllabization.[10] For instance, the words "wrong" and "our" in line 34 sound like "wro-o-ng" and "ow-wer" when delivered by Anderson. The two words scan in the following approximate manner:

wro-o-ng   ou-r

Subformula 1, of the Anderson formula illustrated above, scans as follows:

34   What-ss wro-o-ng with ou-r ti-mes

35   Whats good or bad in ti-mes like thee-zz

36 Whats good children-ah

37 Or what is ba-ad

Unfortunately, the scansions above exaggerate the speech pattern, but lines 34 and 35 do scan to nine syllables each, line 36 to four syllables, and line 37 to five syllables.

The next seven lines, lines 38–44, do not exhibit syllabic extension, but can be scanned according to inflection, suggesting tone contours. The lines are contoured as follows:

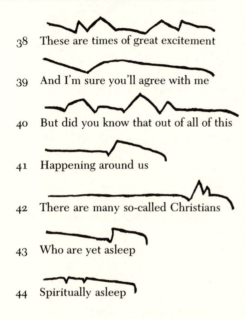

38 These are times of great excitement

39 And I'm sure you'll agree with me

40 But did you know that out of all of this

41 Happening around us

42 There are many so-called Christians

43 Who are yet asleep

44 Spiritually asleep

The style changes suggested by this rough and very approximate notation system are noteworthy. That is, the secular portion of the formula manifests a staccato style, while the sacred portion of the formula takes a more even contoured oral style. While those "style changes" are not as marked in the other of Anderson's formulas as they are in this one, the pattern is persistent enough to indicate that it may be Anderson's way of supporting and identifying the sacred/secular polarities in his sermon formulas.

Another technique used commonly in the performance of the African-American sermon, and in forms of African-American music, is melisma, or the production of several notes around one syllable. Melisma is generally known as an ornamental style in Indian and Asian musics and, I am advised, Italian opera as well. It is also identified in the singing styles of traditional and contemporary African-American performers, such as Aretha Franklin, James Cleveland, and Albert King. As a sermonic device, it is used most frequently in extending syllables and words. At its most expressive level, it accompanies heightened affect in sermon performance.

The dramatic pause and emphatic repetition in which the base phrase formula, usually a free-clause formula, is repeated with increasing intensity or varied tones, are additional techniques employed by the African-American preacher in shaping spoken phrases and formulas into an irrhythmic unit.[11]

The African-American sermonic unit, then, can be considered as oral formula. In addition to being a "group of hemistich phrases shaped into an irrhythmic metric unit when performed to express an aspect of a central theme," the sermonic formula must also evidence a tension between secular and sacred polarities. Each formula, while developing an aspect of the central theme, is directly related to the preacher's announced topic.

This unit construction notion in the development of the sermon in part answers the query concerning a good or successful sermon and a sermon which is less than successful.[12] The well-preached sermon fully develops its constituent formulas and formulaic structures. Metaphorical images are fully drawn, Bible verses are stated and interpreted, ideas are presented abstractly and applied concretely, exempla and other generic forms are used as full sequences in the sermon, and the preacher moves progressively from one formula to the next through transitional free clauses.

By comparison, the less successfully preached sermon strings together images sketchily drawn, summarizes biblical verses rather than exploring them as narrative subjects, avoids the use of exempla, and tends to have fewer well-developed formulas than the well-preached sermon. Illustrative of the less successfully preached sermon are Anderson's two sermons that are under consideration here.

E.   Closure is rarely found at the end of the African-American sermon. The sermon is open-ended and compares favorably with Abrahams's finding on the open-ended nature of African-American performance forms generally.[13] For example, closure as final and summary statements of the sermon are missing from the final lines of the following sermons.

CLEVELAND SERMON NO. 1

272   Put yourself in the right hand of God
      And He will raise you up
274   God resents the powerful and gives grace to the humble
275   Bow your heads now where you are now

CLEVELAND SERMON NO. 2

[Final exemplum in the sermon concerning preparedness for the
life of a Christian. Exemplum: Bishop Cleveland and two fellow
passengers are nervous about a flight from Los Angeles to San
Francisco. Cleveland's passengers are drunk and full of fear for having put their faith in the bottle. Cleveland puts his faith in prayer
and has few fears. The plane arrives safely.]

346   Come let us pray now

ANDERSON SERMON NO. 1

229   Let me tell you the Gospel is the only thing that will save
         your
      Dying soul
231   Oh yes
232   For the Gospel is the power

ANDERSON SERMON NO. 2

239   But when I found the Lord
240   I found joy
      Yeah, joy
      Yeah, joy was found
      I found joy
244   Peace to my dying soul

These illustrations of the termination of the performed African-
American sermon strongly suggest that the preacher's personal testimony is used to end the sermon. Symbolically, the preacher assumes
the burden of commitment and example for his congregation. As well,
the stating of the polarities of the sermon takes place in the closing
lines. Although there is a strong sense that the sermon has concluded a
phrase, its energy carries into a time-space well beyond the limitations
imposed by the performing place and time. The actual performance will
continue its energy, its sensibility, in the daily lives of the congregation.
    These five categorizations of the units of the African-American
sermon make up the infrastructure of the genre. They are the "build-

ing blocks" that provide a cohesive strength for the sermon. Each of these units is obligatory and will most frequently follow the order in which they are discussed here.

The Exemplum in the Performed African-American Sermon

The exemplum is such a common feature in the construction of the sermon that the nature of its presence and the character of its form are deserving of an independent consideration. Regarding the exemplum in African-American narrative performance, J. Mason Brewer wrote:

> In medieval Europe, short narratives employed to illustrate or confirm a moral were called "exempla." Indeed, the use of the exemplum in the pulpit by churchmen became such a vogue in the 14th century that serious opposition was registered against it by Chaucer, Dante, John Wycliffe, and other writers. . . . Although a protest against its use caused it to suffer rapid decline in the sixteenth century, the exemplum remained in use both in England and on the European continent. . . . It was in the U.S., however, that the conditions necessary to bring the exemplum back into vogue rose again. . . .
>
> The term "preacher tale" was widely used by Negroes when referring to the religious anecdote. It included stories told by preachers in the pulpit and those related about preachers. . . . Although now in a period of decline as a pulpit device, preacher tales are still in the living tradition of Negroes. . . .
>
> Granted that Negro religious tales fail in many instances to conform to the pattern of the traditional exempla and fall short of the requirements that would qualify them to be classified with the moralizing, or illustrative, tale of antiquity, it must still be conceded that they have one characteristic in common with that particular genre of folk narrative—the attribute of entertainment.[14]

Brewer was confusing the nature of the exemplum as genre and the nature of the "preacher tale" as an ethnic category because he failed to recognize the distinctive utilization of the exemplum in African-American narrative performance. Brewer's "preacher tales" are a multigenre category of materials grouped around a subject, the African-American preacher. The "religious anecdote" of Brewer's mention can be joke or personal narrative, rap, or any of several other folkloric forms, including that specific category folklorists recognize as the folktale, that is, the preacher tale.

By using the classification "religious anecdote" for preacher tale, Brewer was able to place the African-American sermon alongside its European analogue. Witnessing the apparent decline of the exemplum in African-American sermon performance, Brewer adduced that the factors which presaged the decline of the exemplum in European traditions were applicable to African-America. That is, the African-American exemplum went into decline as entertainment factors became more commonplace in the performance of the form. In this finding, Brewer positioned himself comfortably in the scholarly tradition that chronicled the decline of the exemplum in Europe. Paul Meyer, Thomas F. Crane, Laurits Boedker, J. Thomas Welter, and Frederich C. Tubach each concluded that the exemplum fell into decline, during the period studied, when it moved from sacred to popular use. Tubach writes, "In allowing the criterion of entertainment to determine the choice of exempla the advocates of this narrative genre unwittingly sowed the seeds for the contamination of the exemplum. It was only a matter of time until the entire exemplum-tradition became an object of attack and derision, and its ultimate decline followed." [15] An interesting note is offered by Boedker in his contention that the exempla were intended for popular use from their very beginning. Boedker argues, "The Dominicans and Franciscans raised the exemplum to a narrative art which would collect listeners everywhere, in streets and marketplaces, at fairs and crossroads, in precincts of churches and inside them. Migrant preachers became strong competitors of more secular artists; jugglers, trouveres, and minstrels." [16] How does a form decline when its use was adopted by the very people for whom it was intended? Apparently, scholars mark the decline of the exemplum as of the time when control of its usage was passed from persons of privileged rank to the general populace.

For both Tubach and Brewer, the shift in function and performance environment was sufficient to declare the exemplum in decline. Tubach was reporting on medieval exempla. It may be that the popularization of the form did significantly alter the structural characteristics of the exemplum. But the rationale for Brewer's conclusion is not as clear. Brewer reports that although in a period of decline, "preacher tales" continue to be told from the pulpits of African-American preachers and in African-American homes. They are as commonly related on street corners, buses, and trains as they are told in barber shops and bars, by church and nonchurch folk alike. The problem for Brewer lay in his imprecision in defining the exemplum in the African-American context. Preacher tales may very well function as exempla; all African-American exempla are not preacher tales.

The exemplum is a customary part of the African-American sermon. Brewer writes that the appearance of the exemplum in America parallels the propagation of Methodism by François Asbury and

Lorenzo Dow in the late eighteenth and nineteenth centuries.[17] It is doubtful that Brewer meant that the exemplum in African-American pulpit use is either archaic or European. His observation is that a narrative technique and form, familiar to African-Americans in a secular context, had a European analogue in the exemplum tradition. It was the European form that came to the attention of scholars who, of political necessity, ascribed early African-American pulpit anecdotal forms to the role of mimicry.

Gerhard Kuttner's outline of the eleven essential characteristics of the exemplum is useful in defining the form generically. The exemplum, notes Kuttner, exhibits the following characteristics:

1. Short passage in prose
2. Narrative progression
3. In most cases is told in the past tense
4. Forms a complete unit: beginning, middle and end
5. Functional elements play important part in determining form
6. Illustrates a moral or religious truth or throws light on society at large or on individuals in particular
7. Form is dramatic and is subordinate to a definite goal or aim; epic details, such as descriptive elaboration, usually omitted or reduced to barest minimum
8. Economy essential and nonessential narrative components like references to specific time and place usually suppressed
9. Specific incident is placed within a general framework in order to increase its universal applicability
10. Employs introductory formulas
11. Element of "atmosphere" absent in most exempla[18]

For the African-American preacher the most important consideration is that the exemplum be illustrative. Bishop Cleveland's view is straightforward on this point: "The people need stories sometimes to bring a point home." Actually, Cleveland's use of the exemplum is more pragmatic than he indicates in this remark.

As the sermon is developed in performance, the African-American preacher is constantly under pressure to anchor his text in a contemporary reality. The sermon itself continually shifts in reference frame from sacred to secular, secular to sacred contexts. This tension, identified previously, pulsates throughout the African-American sermon and gives a sermon performance a characteristic immediacy and vitality. But it is in the proper use of the exemplum that the tension spoken of earlier finds resolution. The two "worlds" that are, in fact, symbiotic become complementary in the exemplum.[19] As a functional device, the use of the exemplum often signals the winding down of the sermon and frequently precedes the movement of the sermon into secular environments, or summation. As an illustration, the following exemplum is taken from Cleveland's "You're Just Not Ready" sermon.

193 There's a little boy
      In Chicago
195 His grandmother's quite a friend of ours
      And she was telling me
      She said
      "You know what?
      My daughter-in-law was having this little boy to pray
200 She was having prayer meeting with the little boy every night
      And she'd take turns and say
      Johnny, tonight's your turn
      You lead the prayer
      And he lead the prayer
205 And the next night
      She say, Jimmy you lead the prayer
      And he would lead the prayer
      And come this here boy at night
      All right son, now you lead the prayer
210 She said, it's your time to pray
      Little boy looked at her
      Kind of sarcastic
      A little deceitful looking grin, half-grin on his face
      Said, 'Listen
215 Suppose there ain't nobody up there
216 And we just hollering up there for nothing?'"

Following the telling of this exemplum, Cleveland opens the next formulaic unit with an interpretation of the exemplum. He begins in line 217,

      I say
      See what the devil done told that boy already?
      A whole lot of folks done decided
220 There's somebody up there.

In another exemplum, which comes at the conclusion of Cleveland's "He Wants Your Life" sermon, he illustrates the need to entrust one's life to Christ:

321 Getting on the plane this evening in Los Angeles
      To come up here

And they packed and jammed that big old seven-oh-seven
It was packed and jammed
325 And there was two fellas come out with me
And was coming and was way back in the line
And says
I say, look, all those folks gonna get on this plane
I said, Can you imagine
330 All these folks gonna get up in the air
Swinging with nothing under them
And one of the fellas said to me
Said, you a preacher
335 He said, How you know you was called to preach
I said, How I know I was called
I say, the way I know I was called
The Bible said that God out of Jesus
The Bible say that He endowed Him with the Holy Ghost and
     with power
340 Who went about doing good and healing all that was oppressed by
     the Devil
I said, Listen have you known young folks to be given up to
     murder until they would kill
A man
You can tell they been drinking
[*Next lines unclear*]
345 . . . [*unclear*] prayer on the plane
346 Come let us pray now

This particular exemplum is less convincing than the preceding one, in
large part because Bishop Cleveland is obviously searching for a dramatic yet efficient tag line. He never quite discovers one, so he simply
invites the congregation to join him in prayer to conclude the sermon.

These two exempla demonstrate the important ways in which the
African-American exemplum differs from its European analogue as
cataloged by Kuttner:

1. Primary concern of exemplum is to anchor, give force and
    presence to, reality
2. Narrative tense is present perfect, fixing the event in the im-
    mediate past
3. Absence of introductory formulas
4. Time and place are important markers
5. Narrative beginnings frequently marked by change in tone;
    closure not usually provided within the exemplum

These characteristics are useful in describing the African-American exemplum. But they are useful in another way as well. Kuttner's categorizations are broad enough to cover any of several narrative forms included in some sermons. Narciss, for instance, regularly uses the Lord's Prayer and the Hail Mary as if they were exempla. Anderson will "read" lyrics of well-known gospel or hymnal-derived songs to illustrate points of faith. On the face of it these are exempla, at least in function, and are so regarded by the preachers mentioned. They are narratives of Christian illustration and example. But are they exempla?

A set of distinctions has been advanced on the nature and form of the African-American exemplum that excludes Anderson's use of song text or biblical stories and Narciss's antiphonal reading of set pieces of liturgy. The factors of time and temporal displacement are critical considerations in the generation of exempla in the course of the performance of the sermon. In order that the generated exemplum "make sense" it must pulsate with the quality Kent described as "is-ness,"[20] a particular contemporaneity which identifies the experience spoken of during the sermon in a secular workaday context. It must be recognizable in terms of the quality of the lived experiences of African-American congregations.

The nonclosure notion, a feature of African-American performance generally, is observable in the African-American exemplum. The "ending" of the exemplum, in African-American sermon performance, does not occupy a space within the performance of the exemplum narrative. Closure occurs at some point during the interpretation and application of the illustrative exemplum, which may be weeks after its initial generation, particularly if it was well received by the congregation.

When Brewer observed that "Negro religious tales fail in many instances to conform to the pattern of the traditional exempla and fall short of the requirements that would qualify them to be classified with the moralizing, or illustrative, tale of antiquity," he was correct, at least in a sense. But finally, the African-American exemplum was not developed from a European model (and should probably have another generic designation), so it should not be surprising that there are substantial differences in the two forms.

The illustrative, moralizing narrative is certainly not new to African-derived folklore systems. Fables which were so prevalent in African narrative systems antedated the appearance of the medieval exemplum by several centuries. Brewer, Tubach, Welter, and Kuttner were all premature in declaring the decline of the exemplum in Anglo-European-American, European, and African-American contexts. It is clear that the exemplum tradition is alive and well in African-American preaching and secular folklore systems. The African-American form differs markedly from the European-American exemplum form and yet shares enough of the general characteristics of the genre to be classified under the exemplum rubric, at least for the time being.

NARRATIVE FUNCTIONS OF AFRICAN-AMERICAN SERMON UNITS

The structural units of the African-American sermon have dynamic, functional capabilities in addition to the characteristics I have described. In this discussion of the narrative functions of the sermon's formulaic units, particular attention will be paid to those which serve referential and evaluative functions.[21]

The terms "referential" and "evaluative" and several others in this discussion are drawn from Labov's and Waletzky's treatment of African-American narratives of personal experience. There are, however, significant differences in the use to which these terms are applied by Labov and Waletzky and the application of the terms in this study of performed African-American sermons. Labov and Waletzky are concerned with identifying narrative strategies for recapitulating personal experiences, especially strategies which match the temporal sequences of recapitulated experiences. They are concerned also with the impact of social context on experienced events and the retelling of those experiences. "The basic narrative units that we wish to isolate," note Labov and Waletzky, "are defined by the fact that they recapitulate experience in the same order as the original events."[22]

For Labov and Waletzky, a narrative's referential function is closely related to the temporal sequence employed in the recapitulation of an experienced event. In this present analysis of African-American sermons, referential function is prescribed by a different set of constraints, although for the most part a "sequence of events" is the sine qua non of the referential formula in the sermon. For instance, in Cleveland's "You're Just Not Ready" sermon we find the following formula unit:

```
        144   Hallelujah

 A      145   God told Joshuay
              I'll be with you just like I was with Moses
              And I'll never let Moses lose the battle
              My God
              Won every battle he had
        150   Ever since he left Egypt
              And I'm doing the same thing for you
              And I'll tell you what
```

153   Joshuay went along all right for a while

*B*¹   154   But listen
155   Somebody got messed up with the cat
And went to stealing
Five suckers went to stealing
Ten suckers went to stealing
And they stole a Babylonian golden [*unclear*]
160   A Babylonian garment of golden [*unclear*]
And hid it in the camp
162   And went to battle

*B*²   163   And lost the battle
And they take to they heels
165   And come back

*B*³   166   And my God
Joshuay say
What's the matter
And they say
170   We couldn't stand before the face of our enemy
If we hadn't took to our heels
172   You'd never see us no more

*B*⁴   173   Joshua said
God, you done done what you said you would never do
175   You said you'd never let me down
[*unclear*]
Everywhere I put my foot on it
[*unclear*]
[*unclear*]
180   Wouldn't be able to stand before my face
As long as they live
Hide me from my shame
183   [*unclear*]

C   184   God said, "Get up from here
185   The fault ain't in Me
There is a Babylonian god
That's stolen back in the camp
I can't work with nobody stealing
Say yeah
190   You know you done told lies
So don't get down and pray
192   You gonna be beating your gums for nothing"

This referential sermon formula refers to a sequence of related events, designated by alphabetical and numerical subscripts. Still, unlike the narratives of Labov's and Waletzky's study, the referential sermon formula need not be the retelling of an event experienced by the preacher. The preacher must, however, use the active voice in the narration of an event series, even though he could not have experienced the reported event. Abrahams's concept of the "Intrusive I" in African-American narrative performance, related to Odum and Johnson's "Dominant Self" concept in African-American song, is applicable here.[23]

> Throughout the narratives we are conscious of a close relationship between the hero of the tale and the person doing the narrating. In most cases, the point of view is strictly first person, allowing the complete identification of narrator and hero. In others, this identification is put at a slight remove by placing the narration in the third person, but allowing the hero some attribute by which one can identify with the narrator. . . .
>
> The "intrusive I" is a convenient gambit in the narrative game. It allows the narrator two personae at the same time, his own as narrator or commentator and that of the hero. He can unite the two at will if he is artful in his narration; he can also dissociate. It is important in certain stories that he be able to vary his perspective, as there will be actions which he as narrator will not approve, or situations in which he would not want to be found. As opposed to the classic English and Scottish ballads, there is nothing removed, long ago, impersonal about these narratives. Even when the narrator's persona retreats from that of the hero or main character, the narrator remains, intruding as a commentator. The "I" never completely disappears, though it may recede temporarily. Thus any of the battles won, physical or verbal, are won by both the hero and the narrator. Yet he is in such control of this small universe that he can be both protagonist and antagonist in this contest. He directs this battle as well as wins it. The glory is all his and the triumph is more than just a verbal one.[24]

Abrahams's conceptualization helps to isolate yet another of the important characteristics of the referential sermon formula. Unlike the exemplum in the African-American sermon, which usually centers on one episode, the events of the referential sermon formula are serially ordered. The subnarrative units of the referential formula—the referential formula is an integral narrative in its own right—cannot be easily displaced within the narrative unit without significantly altering the semantic interpretation of the unit. The construction, for purposes of illustration, of the above referential unit from Cleveland's key sermon is shown in table 1.

Clearly it is not possible to reorder the segments of this referential

TABLE 1.   Summary of Referential Unit Segments in Cleveland's
"You're Just Not Ready" Sermon

Segment	Corresponding sermon lines	Summary
A	145–53	God tells Joshua that as long as Joshua and his army follow the Commandments they will win every battle, just as Moses, through his faith, overcame all obstacles placed before him and his followers.
B^1	154–61	Members of Joshua's army steal a Babylonian idol and hide it in Joshua's camp before going into battle.
B^2	162–65	Joshua's army loses the battle and is forced to return to the camp in retreat.
B^3	166–72	In reply to his request for a report, Joshua is told that the enemy was simply too overpowering, that Joshua's army had to flee to survive.
B^4	173–83	Joshua repudiates God and claims shame in the face of his army.
C	184–92	God chastises Joshua for his inconstant faith, tells Joshua of the stolen idol back in his camp, restates His principle that He will not work with thieves, and returns responsibility for the lost battle to Joshua.

unit without altering the interpretation of the narrative. The orientation,[25] or introductory segment, A, cannot come after the complicating segment, B^1, if the integrity of the unit as a narrative is to be maintained. The narrative is about the consequences of the lack of faith. Consequently the orientation segment must include the principle that will later be violated and the consequences of the violation. In the case of segment A in this narrative, the principle (faith in God's Commandments) and the consequences (failure to gain desired objectives) are understood by the congregation. Bishop Cleveland does not feel it necessary to specify principle and consequences of principle except to recall the well-known biblical experience of Moses and his flight from Egypt.

The complicating actions of the narrative are designated as B^1 to B^4. Not only must segment A be temporally ordered with respect to the B segments, but each of the B segments must also be temporally ordered with respect to each other. Segment B^1 should precede B^2, which should be followed by B^3 and B^4. The complicating segments of the narrative unit include the application of the principle and the circumstances that provide for the violation of the stated principle.

The final segment of the referential unit in the African-American sermon is reserved for the preacher's commentary on the dilemma that caused the violation of the stated principle. This segment functions as the resolution of the narrative and the statement of the intent of the narrative. Joshua is finally told why his troops failed in battle. They were thieves and idol worshipers. Joshua is then admonished not to deny God because his desires were not realized but to accept responsibility himself for the righting of the situation. The implications for the preacher's congregation are clear: you can achieve worldly and spiritual success through a strong and constant faith in God.

As a narrative device and a narration technique, the referential function is indispensable to a well-performed sermon. The referential unit is an intense encapsulation of those techniques and considerations more expansively employed in the performance of the whole sermon. In its most formal aspects, the referential unit of the African-American sermon is an independent narrative structure within the larger sermon performance.

In addition to the orientation, the complicating, and the resolution, or termination, segments of the African-American sermon structure and the sermon formulaic units, there is the evaluation segment. Another sermonic narrative function, utilized both as a formulaic unit and a subformula phrase, the evaluation formula is complementary to the referential sermonic unit. Labov and Waletzky regard the importance of the evaluative function in the personal experience narrative in the following manner:

> We would like to suggest that a narrative which contains an orientation, complicating action and the result is not a complete narrative. It may carry out the referential function perfectly, and yet seem difficult to understand. Therefore it is necessary for the narrator to delineate the structure of the narrative by emphasizing the point where the complication has reached a maximum: the break between the complication and the result. Most narratives contain an evaluation section which carries out this function.[26]

Labov and Waletzky also note that the evaluation of a narrative is "that part of the narrative which reveals the attitude of the narrator towards the narrative by emphasizing the relative importance of some narrative units as compared to others."[27]

Following the exemplum (sermon lines 193–216) in Cleveland's

"You're Just Not Ready" sermon concerning the friend of a little Chicago boy who questions the existence of God, Cleveland preaches,

217 I say
See what the devil done told that boy already?
A whole lot of folks done decided
220 There's somebody up there
Hallelujah
You may not know it
May not ever know it
But its somebody up there
225 But you just ain't ready for Him
Yes
He just ain't ready to answer
My God
Hallelujah to God
230 And so when you go to criticize and
Say there's nothing to it
And God don't answer prayer
And these folks are lying when they say God give them this
And that God give them that
235 Before you do that
You get ready
237 Before you get caught

(This evaluation formula precedes the sermon's resolution formula, sermon lines 238–257.)

The evaluation formula in the performed African-American sermon is marked by the preacher's abandonment of the "intrusive I" technique, during which the preacher places himself in the temporal environment of the event being described, and the assumption of his own narrative persona. While the preacher uses such a shift to summarize the preceding illustrative examples of the sermon's theme, or to "make the lesson clear," as Cleveland remarked, it has a more direct function in the sermon performance. The congregation needs to be reminded of the presence and personality of the preacher as the experienced teacher and leader of his flock.

SOUND AND THE PERFORMED AFRICAN-AMERICAN SERMON

Units of nonarticulated sound are keys to understanding the organizing principles of the African-American sermon. Sound, either articulated as in the spoken word or nonarticulated but voiced, serves as the foundation for the performance of the African-American sermon and is regarded in these pages as a sermon event equal in importance to word phrases.[28]

The production and quality of sound phrases, and the identification of sound-phrase generating principles, are critical aspects of this analysis of African-American performed sermons. Sound can be said to have value or cognitive worth in a sermon performance and can be linked to affective referents. In this sense, sound is symbolic. Cognitive sound symbols, or sermonphones, are the principal vehicles for the movement of ideas in the preaching of sermons. The production of certain sound characteristics by the preacher can be correlated with affective responses on the part of members of the congregation, and it therefore becomes possible to measure the production of sound and the physical contours of sound in the preached sermon to determine whether nonarticulated sound carries affect and meaning.

Walter Ong's comments on the nature of oral events in culture help to focus this discussion:

> The world of a dominantly oral . . . culture . . . is dynamic . . . , an
> event world rather than an object world. What we are getting at here
> can be understood in terms of the nature of sound as compared to other
> sensory perceptions. Sound is of itself necessarily an event in the way in
> which the object of no other sense is. Sound signals the use of power,
> since sound must be in active production in order to exist at all. . . .
> It tells us something is going on . . . hearing registers force, the dy-
> namic. . . . Moreover, voice is for man the paradigm of all sound, and to
> it all sound tends to be assimilated. . . . The dynamism inherent in all
> sound tends to be assimilated to the dynamism of the human being. . . .
>   The larger conceptual and verbal structures in which oral-aural
> man stores what he knows consists in great part of stories that turn on
> human action and on the interaction of man and man.[29]

Ong's conceptualization of sound activity in a cultural matrix has been important in informing my approach to describing the nature of nonarticulated speech in the performance of the African-American sermon.

A significant correlation is observable in African-American sermon performance between a preacher's nonarticulated sound phrasing at the affective height of his preaching and the most expressive response on the part of the congregation. Rosenberg, Davis, and Crowley have represented this phenomenon as evidence of the emotional nature of African-American preaching.[30] But African-American congregations are not driven to uncontrollable frenzy at these times of seeming emotional abandon. And certainly African-American congregations do not suspend judgment, even during the most affective part of the preaching. Frequently, a preacher will abruptly terminate his incantative phrasing in response to a caution voiced by a respected member of the congregation, sent and received above the seeming din of a church gripped by passion and ecstasy. Or the preacher may shift a philosophical or cosmological emphasis if disapprobation is expressed by either the Amen or Deacon corners of the church. "Sound" manifested during an African-American sermon is not "noise." Community-determined ideas and values are communicated in the coded sound channels of the sermon event. And the concurrent coding and decoding processes which characterize preacher and congregational oral-aural interaction during sermon segments have philosophical and aesthetic dimensions. This nonarticulated but full voicing is as significant to a congregation's interpretation of the preached sermon as the articulated word.

Ethnophilosophic and ethnoaesthetic considerations are implied in the oral levying of judgment and valuation by African-American congregations in response to preached sermons. Syntactic and philosophic modifications of text and delivery in the preached sermon may result from a congregation's expression of judgment and valuation in the course of the sermon performance. I do not mean to imply that the total sermon performance can be evaluated by oral function criteria. A significant amount of meaning can be derived from a study of nonverbal behavior in the sermon performance environment as well. But so important are the verbal art[31] functions in the preached sermon event that those functions overshadow other modes. For instance, the texture in sermon performance depends on the active and skillful use of sound properties and sermonphones by the preacher.

The sermonphone in African-American sermon performance is a primary concept in this discussion. Sound, at least in the performance of the sermon, is created. An invention of the preacher and members of his congregation, it implicates history as well. As invention, the sermonphone concept also implies intention and function. That is, the preacher or his congregation do not generate sound at random and without regard for historical precedent, appropriateness, and the politics of affect. The preacher or members of his congregation are engaged in a series of determinations and valuations before voicing a sermonphone. If, as Ong maintains, the voice is "the paradigm of all sound," it is because the voice produces qualities that can be identified as part of a group cognition system, essentially an ethnohermeneutic structure in this instance.[32] It is in this cognitive system that the concept of African-American sermonphones becomes intelligible.

David Strauss's report on the interaction of phonic qualities and "memory" in music performance is usefully considered here:

> Tone color is also affected by tempo. By varying the speed of the music the composer [or preacher] permits the onset and decay overtones to have more or less time to affect the listener. . . . A quickly played passage seems less rich in tone than the same passage played more slowly.
>   This related to the process of aural "scanning." The ear "remembers," quite unconsciously, tones for some time after they are heard. The ear "scans" the time axis of the music and evaluates tone combinations in terms of the predecessors and successors. . . . This, as well as most of the complex processes by which one finds meaning and sense in music, depends clearly on the process of "aural scanning."[33]

If, as Strauss seems convinced, sound phrases are more "rich" or evocative when elongated through a temporal space, then the custom of African-American performers, including preachers, of sustaining, or "worrying" tones through melismatic phrasings becomes more than a mere mechanical technique. Aural scanning becomes a dynamic principle of African-American sermonphone production with a strong import for the discovery of nonwritten historical documents in the sermon event. The notion of a "race memory" may still be very much a matter of inquiry. Yet, the suggestion being made here is that some faculty, some survival sense experienced communally and best understood phenomenologically, has been critical in the preservation of certain cognitive "ideas" in the performed African-American sermon event. Many of these "ideas" are couched in sermonphone production.

This idea is readily observable in African-American music performance. In improvisational music, so-called jazz, Miles Davis, John Coltrane, Thelonius Monk, Cecil Taylor, B. B. King, and many others are able to generate emotive sounds—joy, pain, love, lover-departed, intercourse—through the manipulation of the range and sound quality of their instruments. African-American audiences "hear" the sounds emanating from the performer and his sensibilities. As the sounds are interpreted, the interpretive medium is not limited to the artistry of the performer, although craft and style are always appreciated, but also includes the ability of the artist to "get down," to discover sonorities, qualities which may assist an audience in reliving an experience. There is, of course, a dual interpretive process going on at these times. The performer is generating a sound series through his own sensibilities around an event or event series. The hearer accepts or rejects the performer's offering, first as it is offered and second as the hearer evaluates the performer's "message," in accordance with the hearer's own interpretation of the expressed experience.

Further investigation using more sophisticated physics research techniques and methods will possibly confirm that sound provides the definitive structure for African-American sermon performance. Such speculation, however, is moving this discussion beyond its narrowly defined purpose: to explore the dimension and nature of sermon-phones in the performed African-American sermon.

To understand and evaluate physical characteristics of sound in an African-American sermon performance, portions of taped sermons were fed through sound evaluation devices. Allowing for the relatively crude interpretive structures used in these explorations and the loss of significant highs and lows in the initial tape of the sermons, some useful determinations were derived from the procedure. Physicists, electronic music composers, and folklorists can profit from these findings by joining forces to understand more of the psychocultural dimensions of sound in African-American narrative performance.

The first phase of the experiment involved feeding portions of the tape of Bishop Cleveland's "You're Just Not Ready" sermon through a sound analyzer constructed by electronic music composer Daniel Goode to measure frequency and frequency balance.[34] Even with compensation, this particular tape taken from a radio broadcast lacked the quality necessary to realize conclusive data. The response measured between 60 and 620 hertz, evidencing the absence of higher frequency contours. This circumstance owed to poor quality transmission of the sermon over reduced-frequency airwaves and distortions inherent in a radio-to-microphone cabling during the initial taping.

More satisfactory results were obtained with a Kay Type B/65 Sonagram, a machine used by Rutgers University ornithologists to measure the quality and characteristics of bird sounds.[35] Unfortunately, this particular machine can handle the equivalent of only ten seconds of taped material, so that an analysis of the entire sermon would have produced more data than could be managed without the aid of specially designed computer programs. To compensate for this, I determined that the most affective and the least affective portions of the sermon would be put through the Kay Sonagram. The results suggest that most sermon activity takes place within the range of 50 to 4,000 kilocycles with approximately 80 percent of that activity taking place in the range of 500 to 2,500 kilocycles. For purposes of comparison, low-frequency telephone transmission takes place at approximately 200 kilocycles. Since the human hearing mechanisms can comfortably handle sound between 16 and 20,000 cycles per second, with the threshold of feeling and involuntary response encountered at 4,000 to 6,000 cycles per second, it seems reasonably clear that the pitch of sermon sounds may not be the generating agency for affective response in the performance of the African-American sermon.

While these data do not conclusively support the contention that there is strong correlation between sermonphone production in African-American preaching and aural-psychological impact on the congregation, some important data can be isolated:

1. Intentional, preacher-produced, nonarticulated sound, including sound-absent phrases, carry a semantic function in the context of African-American sermon performance

2. While the production of sermonphonic units by the preacher is significant enough (at plus 4,000 kilocycles) to engage involuntary oral-psycho-physiological response on the part of members of a congregation, it is not significant enough to induce frenzy and reality suspension

3. Preacher-produced sermonphones, and the aesthetic principles that generate preacher-produced sound/semantic units (sermonphones), may be closer to the structures that support African-American improvisation than to narrative creative invention

4. Congregational interpretation of preacher-produced nonarticulated sound is possible through what is essentially an affective, ethnohermeneutic system composed of physical, cultural, social, environmental, and historical "filters"

These four summary findings are obviously not an exhaustive listing of the information to be gleaned from an analysis of the nature of sound in African-American sermon performance. The purpose of this section is to make recommendations for future areas of inquiry, based on a utilization of sound physics and sound evaluation devices. More specifically, I suggest that this important research needs the combined talents of folklorists, linguists, physicists, and computer science humanists.

One of the tasks of such a research team might be the clarification of the phenomenological characteristics of the sermonphone. At this point in the research, the sermonphone is a qualitative unit of sound in the performed African-American sermon. The emphasis of this characteristic is on the quality and "personality" of the sound unit and not on any measurement that the notion of "unit" would seem to indicate. The sermonphone is not synonymous with such standard units of measurement as feet, inches, or meters. As a practical matter, a sermonphone may be a word or a group of words, a nonarticulated sound or a sound-absent phrase (not to be confused with a pause). Consider the following sermonphone illustrations:

1. *One-word sermonphones.* One of the most frequently used and best-known sermonphones is the monosyllabic "well." When the spirit of the Lord has been visited upon a preacher in the course of performing the most affective part of his sermon, he may take a few steps back from the pulpit, seeming to "cool out," to settle himself. If the church is convinced the preacher is experiencing a genuine visitation, someone in the congregation might intone "well." Other members of the congregation may pick this up and turn the word into a litany, gradually diminishing the hold of the passion of the visitation. (This diminishing of strong emotion may also take place if members of the congregation are "taken" deeply moved following a powerful sermon performance or a choir selection to the extent the progress of the worship service is slowed.) At these times, "well" is repeated and chanted and has the effect of bringing the church together into a unified, experiencing community.

2. *Phrase sermonphones.* Phrase sermonphones are more specialized than one-word sermonphones. Phrases such as "preach it," "tell it," "thank you, Jesus," or "carry me, Lord," are generally used in a supportive manner to affirm an observation of the preacher or a particular event in the church or sermon. Like the one-word sermonphone, the phrase sermonphone heavily connotes a prior experience, either historically when the group is implicated, or individually, when a phrase seems quite peculiar to a personal experience. Phrase sermonphones rarely carry the affect of the one-word sermonphone and are rarely passed to an entire community or congregation during a worship service.

3. *Nonarticulated sermonphones.* In his study, Mitchell notes the prevalence of this particular feature, although he simply refers to it as a "stylistic feature," noting that it is the "stereotypical use of a musical tone or chant in preaching. Mitchell goes on to indicate that nonarticulated sermonphones are "referred to as 'mooning,' 'mourning,' 'whooping,' 'turning,' 'zooming'"[36] The nonarticulated sermonphones are used at that point in the sermon performance when articulated words are inappropriate to the quality of the affect requiring expression and may consist of highly stylized, and easily recognized,

grunts, groans, and hums. Of the four classes of sermonphones, this class is the literal representation of the quasi
function of the sermonphone.

4.   *Sound-absent sermonphones.* Since the presence of sound is
the sine que non of this consideration of the classes of sermonphones in African-American sermon performance, this category would seem to be inappropriate to this discussion. Yet in
all respects, this category satisfies the sermonphone class
tests, save the perceived sensation of sound reception. Certainly the sound-absent sermonphone is more difficult to perceive than the other three classes, but its markers are readily
apparent. When a preacher, or a member of the congregation,
frequently during the most affective part of the sermon
performance, introduces a motion of the mouth that should
result in a sound but does not, but is clearly "heard" by a
congregation, the initiating party is said to have generated
a sound-absent sermonphone. In point of fact, the sound-
absent sermonphone shares the distinction of being considered a paralinguistic aspect of proxemic actions and events.
But since sound is the qualifying entity in this discussion, the
sound-absent sermonphone is considered a semantic category.

The quality that makes these four events a related group is the
symbolic representation, in sound, of semantic functions. While the
sermonphone classes are organic to speech events, they are super-
semantic with respect to speech event functions. Sermonphones are
cognitive symbol systems and can be used to evoke historical ideas and
contemporary circumstance. The sermonphone, to paraphrase Armstrong, is an expression of power, of control over the events of one's life,
and has the power to reinvent and relive portions of an earlier experience that may yet have significance in the life of the group or
individual.[37]

The dimensions of sermonphone production are, for the time
being, locked into the mysteries of the workings of the mind. When
scientists have begun to understand more of the impact of sound use in
cultural performance, then this exploration will proceed apace. Until
that time, the folklorist must content himself or herself with the knowledge that while sound figures prominently in African-American sermon performance, its precise character has yet to be identified.

The foregoing series of analytic and descriptive perspectives on
the constituent elements of the performed African-American sermon

makes possible an evaluation of the quality of a performed sermon. While African-Americans have little trouble identifying an especially well performed sermon, the articulation of the standards by which sermon performances are measured are not as easily arrived at. The preceding discussions in this chapter offer an approach to the structural and semantic considerations that make up the ethnohermeneutic system utilized by African-Americans in the interpretation and appreciation of the performed sermon. More important, it is hoped that they will help students of African-American expressive culture understand more fully the question of aesthetics in the performance of folklore materials.

An African-American sermon is constructed of narrative units, at least four, that can exist independently of the sermon verbal mold. These "independent" units may manifest formal folkloristic structures, as in the case of the exempla, or derive their basic properties from the functions of the units in the sermons. That is, a group of phrases that depict a coordinated series of events is an evaluative sermon formula. A group of related clauses in which the preacher assumes an active narrative voice—and adopt several personnae—may be considered a sermon resolution formula. Other obligatory units and characteristics that can be used to define the performed African-American sermon will be employed in the following chapter when a sermon is subjected to a full analysis to test the validity of the findings of this study.

Chapter Four
The Testing of the Performed African-American Sermon Model

What is a successful sermon? What is a less-than-successful sermon? The Reverend Carl Anderson's "Ezekiel and the Vision of Dry Bones" is a narrative tour de force. It is a superior illustration of the African-American narrator's skills in generating rich and multiple images from a basic formula structure. And it would certainly seem to fulfill the most pragmatic function of the sermon: to instruct a congregation in the techniques necessary to live a full and Christian life. But on closer examination, Anderson's sermon adheres to the structures and principles of the performed African-American sermon model only minimally. It is a less-than-successful sermon.

The key sermon for this study, Bishop Cleveland's "You're Just Not Ready" sermon is, obviously, a successful sermon. In all respects Cleveland's sermon exhibits those characteristics, in full measure generally, that define the African-American sermon genre. Since the Cleveland sermon is the example from which important considerations of this study have been generated, one would expect that it would be exemplary. That is its purpose. By the definition advanced previously, however, both the Anderson and the Cleveland sermons are African-American sermons. Why, then, is it significant that Anderson has continually to exhort his congregation to respond to his preaching performance and Cleveland does not? If this study has any import at all, it is that now it is possible to state quite precisely why one performance of a narrative form achieves its desired impact while another falls short of its intent.

In the conclusion to his article "Musical Adaptation among Afro-Americans," John Szwed refers to a comment by Lerone Bennett on expressive dichotomies in African-American culture and then offers a summary view of his own:

> Further inquiry may reveal that alternate musical forms not only exist simultaneously but may be more available to individual option than we have so far been led to believe. This may indeed be part of what Lerone

Bennett, Jr., means when he warns against Euro-American interpretations of the Negro tradition: "The essence of the tradition is the
extraordinary tension between the poles of pain and joy, agony and ecstasy, good and bad, Sunday and Saturday. One can, for convenience,
separate the tradition into Saturday (Blues) and Sundays (Spirituals).
But it is necessary to remember that the blues and the spirituals are not
two different things. They are two sides of the same coin, two banks, as
it were, defining the same stream." But whether or not a dichotomous
model of musical social reality is fully applicable to Afro-America, a unified musical form and performance role analysis appears necessary. An
awareness of styles and counter styles in all aspects of expressive culture
should offer us a richer and more realistic picture of the New World
Negro experience.[1]

The quotation from Rev. Wyatt Tee Walker in the epigraph to this book
similarly observes the simultaneity, and crossover, in the sacred and
profane worlds of African-American performance.

In the performed African-American sermon those dichotomies
Bennett considers to be "two banks . . . defining the same stream" on
closer examination appear to be even more complementary. These sacred and profane dichotomies are two surfaces of the same bas-relief.
The background surface can be thought of as the abstract sacred dimension of the sermon narrative. This dimension contains the general,
nonspecific references to churchly ideals, to so-called Christian example, to the intentionally elusive goal of living an existence patterned
after the teachings of Christly doctrine. The relief, more finely etched
with much greater definition, can be said to represent the secular dimensions of the sermon narrative structure. Those illustrations which
are fully, artfully chiseled into strong narrative images, the examples
that are knowingly yanked from street corners, complement the more
subtle, muted textures of the performed sermon's sacred dimensions.

In the actual performance of the African-American sermon the
distinctions between secular dynamic and churchly dimension are
manifest in the very development of the sermon's text. While the
preacher almost casually explicates churchly doctrine and example
during the course of his sermon performance, he carefully and explicitly develops secular illustration and reference. So deliberately does he
engage in the exploitation of secular ideas in his preaching that this
marked emphasis was labeled the "weighted secular factor" in African-
American sermon performance.

The weighted secular factor in the performed African-American
sermon draws upon a strong need for experienced contemporaneity in
the ethnophilosophical structures of the sermon system. Preachers are

not concerned with life in the "hereafter," at least not in a primary sense. Mitchell notes that "the gospel must speak to the contemporary man and his needs [and] . . . Black fathers . . . look for the answer to Black people's needs."[2] Consequently, any definition of the sermon as genre must include this important dynamic.

The African-American sermon has a religious purpose, of that there can be no doubt. Through the sermon the preacher can encourage his congregation to consider the quality of their lives, particularly with respect to sets of principles previously acknowledged to be useful in one's secular existence. In the case of the African-American preacher and his congregation, those principles, in general terms, are closely related to Protestant doctrine. This is the "larger intent" of the African-American sermon definition. And this is why the churchly dimension of the performed sermon is less specific than the secular dynamic. The churchly dimension of the sermon performance serves as a point of reference, as an understood and mutually agreed upon framework. It is not the thrust of the sermon. The environment of the sermon is the world of experience in which people live and love, hate and believe. The sermon's lessons and illustrations must be drawn from the contemporary world and must, in fact, be drawn from contexts familiar to the congregation.

In broad terms, this sociophilosophic context is evidenced by a generalized tension which draws through the whole sermon. In a statement quoted previously, Bennett suggests that the tension in African-American performance operates "between the poles of pain and joy, agony and ecstasy, good and bad, Sunday and Saturday."[3] The "tension" of the performed sermon is not as dramatic as that identified by Bennett, although as Bennett suggests, the tension quality of the sermon is derived from polarity sets. The narrative ideas that are generated as speech events in the performance of sermon systems are balanced between concretely secular and abstractly churchly or sacred perspectives.

Cleveland's "You're Just Not Ready" sermon amply illustrates such bipolar tension. In fact this "tension" is in its most ideal state in the Cleveland sermon. In a virtually parallel construction, Cleveland explicates his theme—the need to be prepared—through concrete examples taken from the secular world and through minimally specified illustrations drawn from a more narrowly perceived sacred canon of behavior. In comparison, Anderson's "Ezekiel and the Vision of Dry Bones" sermon only vaguely exhibits the tension characteristics appropriate to the African-American sermon. Anderson's discourse is on the state of contemporary Christianity and its relative parallels to Babylon

TABLE 2.   Summary of Secular/Sacred Theme-Related Polarities in
Cleveland's "You're Just Not Ready" Sermon

Segment	Lines	Theme	Secular Units	Sacred Units
A	21–92	The need to be prepared	Can't get married, can't get job, etc., without prior preparation	If mental attitude isn't appropriate, God will not grant request for salvation
B	93–139	How to get ready	Have to be able to make down payment	Just have to decide to commit self (to God) to achieve full life
C	140–219	Exemplum to illustrate segment *B*	Boy in Chicago challenges existence of God (just not ready)	Joshua loses battle because of stolen idol worshippers in camp (just not ready)
D	220–64	Reward for those who are prepared	For those ready to accept God, peace in the secular world	(Same as secular unit)

and Judah. Anderson is concerned to lead his congregation to salvation through belief in the Gospel; in point of fact the bulk of the sermon is a near-brilliant example of the African-American narrator's technique. Anderson explores the number three in the lives of Ezekiel and the state of Israel. But Anderson only briefly refers to secular example. For the most part the sermon is replete with abstract, though vivid, images drawn from sacred references.

This bipolar tension is not only a characteristic of the overall narrative structure of the sermon system. The tension is evidenced in the sermon's various constituent narrative units as well. The generalized (or abstracted) sacred elements of a sermon formulaic unit must always appear in the same morphological environment as specifically referenced secular elements. Again, the key sermon typifies this requirement generously. The Anderson sermon does not.

To facilitate this analysis, I have segmented the Cleveland key sermon into units of narrative action based on particular theme-related functions (table 2).

Cleveland is wholly successful in each of the sermon's major narrative units in his use of bipolar tensions to support his systematic examination of the sermon's theme and thematic units. But when the same schema is applied to Anderson's sermon, it becomes clear that the pragmatic development of the sermon's theme is uneven and sparse. Anderson achieves a minimal statement with respect to the utilization of the necessary bipolar tension in the units of the sermon, but each statement is vague and conservative (see table 3).

It must be kept in mind that the point in question is not whether Anderson's sermon is an African-American sermon. Anderson is an African-American preacher and his sermons fall within the requirements for the performed African-American sermon. The query at hand seeks a response to a finer point: why do some African-American sermon performances "work" better than others? How can this difference be best explained? More directly, has the series of analytical perspectives developed in this study reached a level of sophistication which permits an examination of more subtle distinctions in the sermon mode?

Both sermons achieve the characteristic of bipolarities of concrete secular and abstract sacred elements in the overall structure and within each of the sermon's units. It is evident in the Cleveland sermon in abundance and in the Anderson sermon sparsely. This is a minimal finding, but it is significant. What can be stated confidently is that in the absence of this important foundation, it is highly unlikely that performed sermons will be successful.

TABLE 3. Summary of Secular/Sacred Theme-Related Polarities in Anderson's "Ezekiel and the Vision of Dry Bones" Sermon

Segment	Lines	Theme	Secular Units	Sacred Units
A	1–28	Ezekiel and the vision of dry bones: non-practicing Christians	Sin	Salvation through the practice of the Gospel
B	29–163	Consequences of nonbelief	Exiled Israelites	Israel
C	164–244	Contemporary Christianity analogous to Babylon and Judah	Dry bones: destruction of cities unfaithful to God	Whole body: acceptance and practice of Christianity

In an earlier consideration of the characteristics and functions of the African-American sermon's structural units, it was determined that the performed sermon is developed in a consistent, orderly manner requiring adherence to a series of obligatory steps. In table 4 the Cleveland and Anderson sermons are evaluated side by side. Each step realized is a generative threshold for the next step. In the absence of one of the steps, the preacher may move to an alternative developmental system, but in all likelihood that alternative mode will not fall appropriately within the parameters of the performed African-American sermon structure.

The information yield from table 4 is not surprising. Cleveland's sermons are more consistently well developed than Anderson's sermons. Predictably, both preachers do well in the most mechanical parts of the development of the sermon, quoting from the Bible in support of the announced theme.

Step *D* is the most critical point in the development of the performed African-American sermon. It is at this point that the preacher

TABLE 4.   Comparison of Narrative Units in the Cleveland and Anderson Sermons

Step	Cleveland No. 1	Cleveland No. 2	Anderson No. 1	Anderson No. 2
A	+5 (lines 3–5)	+3 (lines 3–4)	−1 (line 20)	+2 (line 21)
B	+2 (lines 30–32)	+5 (line 5)	+4 (lines 12–17)	+4 (lines 8–10)
B^2	+5 (lines 7–32)	+5 (lines 12–13)	+5 (lines 3–11)	+5 (lines 1–10)
C	+5 (lines 33–49)	+3 (lines 14–19)	+4 (lines 29–38)	+0 (lines 29–35)
D	+5 (lines 46–219)	+3 (lines 14–307)	+2 (lines 34–199)	+1 (lines 32–231)
E	+5 (lines 272–75)	+3 (lines 321–46)	+4 (lines 229–32)	+4 (lines 239–44)

Note: *A* = intercession of God or Christ in the generation of the sermon text; *B* = theme identification; B^2 = supporting Bible quotation; *C* = interpretation of Bible quotation; *D* = body of sermon (well-defined units with polarities); *E* = closure. Minus (−) and plus (+) symbols identify the relative absence (−) or presence (+) of a particular characteristic. The numbers 1 to 5 suggest the relative intensity of the characteristic. Thus (+5) suggests that a characteristic has been employed and has achieved its desired impact on the developing structure of the performed sermon. A (−5) would suggest that a characteristic is lacking in some important aspect so as to seriously impair the further development of the sermon.

begins to make his individuating genius apparent. It might be expected that this "genius" would make itself evident at step C, the interpretation of the Bible quotation, since free association and movement away from the rigorous demands of formal sermon development would seem to occur at this point. Step C is more properly the final step in the obligatory phase of the sermon—steps A through C and derives its formal properties from the requirements of the developmental phase to which it belongs.

Still, there is some carryover from step C to step D. It is during step C, for instance, that the preacher establishes his pattern sensibility, and this obviously becomes an important mnemonic device in step D. But it is in step D that the preacher must clearly demonstrate the state of his narrative art and skill. In the first Cleveland sermon, the key sermon, the preacher accomplishes the fullest realization of desirable sermon unit development. The properly constructed sermon is an argument in reasoning. Each unit of the construction must advance the argument. There is, as well, the requirement that each unit must evidence a bipolar tension as it examines an aspect of the sermon argument. Cleveland realizes the requirements of step D with relative ease. His narrative units are balanced between concrete secular and abstract sacred elements and are weighted in favor of the secular elements.

By comparison, Anderson's step D units are poorly defined and imbalanced. In Anderson's second sermon, the units comprising lines 55–150 are wonderfully executed expositions of the number three. They do not, however, carry the semantically balanced function required of the performed sermon narrative unit. And indeed, while the listener is awed by Anderson's narrative skill and his ability to utilize the formula-generating system to great advantage, his congregation is not impressed with the license he takes with the structures of African-American sermon performance. Even though step D is the least formally constructed level of sermon development, there are minimal expectations. That Anderson does not meet them is evidenced in his need to utilize fifty of his sermon's 244 lines to explicitly encourage his congregation to respond to his preaching. The most telling evidence of Anderson's inability fully to employ appropriate sermon narrative technique is in line 173 of his "Dry Bones" sermon. Anderson promises his congregation to "hook this train up in a minute." Not only does Anderson admit his failure to develop the bipolar tension so necessary to the sermon's cohesion and unity, he has not been able to demonstrate convincingly to his congregation that he is "making sense."

The same circumstance is apparent in Anderson's first sermon, "In Times Like These." Of the 232 lines, 39 are given over to explicit solicitation of response. Commonly, African-American preachers encourage congregations to respond to the sermon performance, but rarely should a preacher have to devote as much as one-fifth of his preaching time to response solicitation. After an initial, almost gratuitous, series of exchanges between congregation and preacher, the congregation understands where it is expected to be most responsive during the sermon performance. In Anderson's case, however, the import of the following series of response solicitations seems clear. At line 133, Anderson promises to "hook this train up in a minute." At line 135 he intones "yes my children." By line 139, Anderson seems to be doubting his abilities as he assures himself, if not his congregation, "I know I'm right about it." By line 144, he is literally requesting God's intervention, "Help me Lord." And finally by line 146, there is a resignation of sorts, "Lord, deliver me from a dead church."

Certainly the circumstance just described can be explained in several ways. Perhaps St. John's Missionary Baptist Church is a "dead" congregation. Perhaps Anderson was simply "off" that day. Still, St. John's can be as lively and responsive as any African-American congregation. When a visiting preacher performed well in the pulpit, the congregation was most appreciative. The implication of the description seems clear enough; whatever the state of his skills in times past, the sermons performed by Anderson in this study are not qualitatively illustrative of the full measure of African-American sermon performance.

There is one final "test." On close examination, will the units of the Cleveland and Anderson sermons exhibit the referential and evaluative functions identified in chapter 3? With respect to the key sermon, the query has been answered. The units that were explored amply exhibited both the referential and evaluative functions. That material need not be reexamined here. However, the Anderson "Dry Bones" sermon was not fully considered in chapter 3, and it is therefore important that the sermon be evaluated in terms of the narrative functions of its units.

The referential function of an African-American sermon unit is carried by the following properties: the unit must be organized through a series of related events temporally ordered and narrated in the active "intrusive I" voice. The referential unit should be divided into three subfunctional sections: an *orientation* section, in which a principle to be violated and the consequences of the violation are stated; a *complicating* section, in which the circumstances leading to the violation of the principle are identified; and a *resolution* section, in which the preacher comments on the dilemma that caused the violation of the stated principle.

TABLE 5.   Summary of Narrative Function Segments in Anderson's
"Ezekiel and the Vision of Dry Bones" Sermon

Segment	Lines	Summary
A	16–28	Introductory; no principle statement
B	29–37	Ezekiel's biodata
C	38–42	Ezekiel, self-styled Son of God
C^2	43–45	Stormy prophesy: "one hundred and seventeen times"
D	46–49	Ezekiel's two audiences: exiles and house of Israel
E	50–53	Evaluative: dry Christians in church cannot express religion
F	54–60	Ezekiel's use of allegory and parables
F^2	61–71	Ezekiel's use of symbolic action: divided hair into three parts, representing the Jewish diaspora
G	72–82	Three and seven, significant numbers
H	83–101	Number three examined: heavenly bodies, elements, life forms, animal forms
I	102–105	Noah's three sons
I^2	106–107	Difficulty of preaching to non-Bible readers
J	108–10	Moses hidden for three months
K	111–14	Moses' three life periods
L	115–21	Solomon's temple workers divided into three classes
M	122–24	Daniel prayed three times daily
M^2	125–27	Shadrack, Meshack, Abednego
M^3	128–31	Christ on the mountain with three disciples
M^4	132–47	Building of three tabernacles
N	148–50	Ezekiel divided hair into three parts
O	151–57	Ezekiel's use of other symbols
P	158–64	Ezekiel speaks in parables and saw vision of God in valley of dry bones
Q	165–66	Many valleys in the Lord
R	167–68	Judah and Jerusalem destroyed as a result of lack of faith in God
S	172–204	Ezekiel in the valley of dry bones
T	205–23	Dry church represents "dry" Christians; nightclubs are full of life; evaluative: the need to make a joyful noise to the Lord

To appreciate more fully the incidence of narrative functions in Anderson's sermons, see table 5, in which the complete text of the "Dry Bones" sermon is schematized. From even a cursory examination of the table it is apparent that all of the conditions for the referential function in African-American preaching have not been met by Anderson. The events in the twenty-six segments of the sermon are neither related nor temporally ordered. Aspects of Ezekiel's ministry are a recurring theme, but at times it is difficult to know whether Ezekiel or the number three is at the core of the sermon.

The most basic requirement of the referential function of a sermon narrative unit is that its components be temporally ordered. Each segment of a referential unit should have a zero displacement range. It should not be possible to move the segments to other positions within the unit without significantly altering the semantic interpretation of the unit. Yet in the Anderson sermon, all segments but the last have a displacement range of virtually the entire length of the narrative unit, the sermon.[4] For instance, segment *B* could easily follow segment *D* without significantly altering the interpretation of the two segments:

> *D*   Ezekiel had two audiences
> One real and present, the exiled about him
> And the other the whole house of Israel
> You understand me
>
> *B*   Now this new Ezekiel signifies God's way of thinking
> Ezekiel is known as one of the most mysterious Hebrew prophets
> Yes sir
> And he began, well, as a boy
> He grew up under the influence of Jeremiah
> And he began to prophesy at the age of thirty
> And for twenty-two years preached by the River of Shafar
> At Talabinth
> And history says he died at the age of fifty-two

Similarly, segment *F*[2] could precede segments *O* and *P* without significantly modifying the semantic sense of the overall unit. What Anderson has done is to string a series of images together with little concern for continuity or consistency. Even the introductory segment, *A*, and the terminal segment, *T*, could be placed elsewhere in the sermon without impairing the narrative continuity of the sermon.

Although Anderson does not use the orientation segment, *A*, of the narrative unit to state the principle to be violated during the course of the unit's complicating segments, he does realize a resolution section in which he seems to comment and interpret the meaning of the unit. Still, in failing to employ the structures of the African-American sermon fully in performance, Anderson's sermons are void of significant impact in the lives of his congregation, although the sermon can, minimally, be included under the African-American sermon rubric.

Appendix

The Full Texts of the Sermons

BISHOP E. E. CLEVELAND
SERMON 1
"You're Just Not Ready"

    1   God bless you
          Everybody say Amen
          As I was coming up the street to church tonight
          Prayed as I walked along
    5   The Lord gave me this message
          And I didn't know what the choir was going to sing tonight
          But I wish you'd listen
          Isaiah, the fifty-ninth chapter said
          "Behold,
   10 The Lord's hands are not shortened
          That He cannot save
          Neither His ear heavy
          That He cannot hear
          But your iniquity has separated
   15 Between you and your God
          And your sins have hid His face from you
          That He will not hear
          For your hands are defiled with blood
          Your fingers with iniquity
   20 Your lips have spoken lies
          Your tongue have muttered perverseness
          None call for justice
          Nor any plead for truth
          They trust in vanity
   25 And speak lies
          They conceive mischief
          And bring forth iniquity."
          And you know what the Lord said?
          I want you to repeat after me
   30 The fault
          Is not in the Lord

You are just not ready
God said here in Isaiah, the fifty-ninth chapter
The fault ain't in Me
35 I know you're about to turn atheist
You're about to say there ain't no God
You're just about to say I'm dead
But the fault ain't in Me
You're just not ready
40 For My blessings
Hallelujah to God
Your iniquity have separated between you and your God
And your sins have hid His face from you
You speak lies and perverse things
45 Thank God
And it's because of you that you can't get the blessing
It doesn't mean that you can't get married now
Plenty folks get married
But everybody ain't ready to get married
50 You haven't got your blood test
You haven't got your license
You haven't got your divorce
It's not final
You got six more months to go
55 So you are not ready
To get married
And folks are getting married every day
Glory to God
It don't mean that there are not jobs
60 There are plenty jobs
You go in there and apply for a job
They throw a question or a sheet
In your face
Answer these questions
65 And if you can't answer them
You're just not ready
The job is for the fella that can fill out the application
And answer the question
Plenty colleges and you can get scholarships
70 But everybody can't go to college
'Cause you're just not ready
They go back and pick up that record where you made "B's" and
   "C's" and "D's"

My God
How many times you ducked school
75 You're just not ready
And they got counselors there at school
To keep you from being so disappointed
And come out such a frizzled mess
They say
80 Listen, you go before the counselor
And let him tell you whether or not you ready for college
Let him tell you whether or not you ready to study to be a doctor
    or a lawyer
He'll get your records and say
No, you're just not ready
85 Say, you take home economics
You take agriculture
You go take social work
Go to asking folks how long they been on the welfare?
You are not ready
90 God said
You just not ready
For Me to answer your questions
You are not ready
For Me to give you your request
95 If you get ready
Man, in quicker than the flash of an eye
I'll come while you call
While you just preachin'
I'll answer
100 My God
Get ready
You'll have to go with Me
If you just decide
I'll give you the size of your heart
105 But you got to be ready
Oh, praise God
Hallelujah
Man say,
My God, come down and get what you want
110 Come down and get furniture
Come down and get a car
Come down, low down payment
Come down and get all your vacation clothes

And make a payment when you come back
115 Come back
And a whole lot of folks can't go down there
Because they're not ready
You ain't paid for the stuff you got
Had to garnishee
120 [*unclear*]
You got to get ready
[*unclear*]
And you know you can't do that
'Cause you ain't ready to vote
125 [*unclear*]
But you ain't ready to get it
[*unclear*]
My God, Hallelujah to God
And He wants to give it to you
130 But you ain't ready
Thank God
Come on people
When I was a boy fifty years ago
I heard a prayer
135 [*unclear*]
They said, God
Since I know You is here and answers prayer
I know You heard me and answer my prayer
[*unclear*] is past and gone
140 And I know now You'll hear me
When I pray and pray right
But He didn't hear then 'cause I didn't know what right is
Thank God
Hallelujah
145 God told Joshuay
I'll be with you just like I was with Moses
And I'll never let Moses lose the battle
My God
Won every battle he had
150 Ever since he left Egypt
And I'm doing the same thing with you
And I'll tell you what
Joshuay went along all right for a while
But listen
155 Somebody got messed up with the cat

And went to stealing
Five suckers went to stealing
Ten suckers went to stealing
And they stole a Babylonian golden [*unclear*]
160 A Babylonian garment of golden [*unclear*]
And hid it in the camp
And went to battle
And lost the battle
And they take to they heels
165 And come back
And my God
Joshuay say
What's the matter
And they say
170 We couldn't stand before the face of our enemy
If we hadn't took to our heels
You'd never see us no more
Joshua said
God, you done done what you said you would never do
175 You said you'd never let me down
[*unclear*]
Everywhere I put my foot on it
[*unclear*]
[*unclear*]
180 Wouldn't be able to stand before my face
As long as they live
Hide me from my shame
[*unclear*]
God said, Get up from here
185 The fault ain't in Me
There is a Babylonian god
That's stolen back in the camp
I can't work with nobody stealing
Say yeah
190 You know you done told lies
So don't get down and pray
You gonna be beating your gums for nothing
There's a little boy
In Chicago
195 His grandmother's quite a friend of ours
And she was telling me
She said

You know what?
My daughter-in-law was having her little boy to pray
200 She was having prayer meeting with the little boy every night
And she'd take turns and say
Johnny, tonight's your night
You lead the prayer
And he lead the prayer
205 And the next night
She say, Jimmy you lead the prayer
And he would lead the prayer
And come this here boy at night
All right son, now you lead the prayer
210 She said, it's your time to pray
Little boy looked at her
Kind of sarcastic
A little deceitful looking grin, half-grin on his face
Said, Listen
215 Suppose there ain't nobody up there
And we just hollering up there for nothing?
I say
See what the devil done told that boy already?
A whole lot of folks done decided
220 There's somebody up there
Hallelujah
You may not know it
May not ever know it
But it's somebody up there
225 But you just ain't ready for Him
Yes
He just ain't ready to answer
My God
Hallelujah to God
230 And so when you go to criticize and
Say there's nothing to it
And God don't answer prayer
And these folks are lying when they say God give them this
And that God give them that
235 Before you do that
You get ready
Before you get caught
Because He said
If you get ready
240 Ask what you will

And it shall be granted
If you believe what you praying
[*unclear*]
Bible say, how you gonna believe?
245 Say well, He's Jesus of Nazareth
You just not ready
And how I'm gonna get ready Brother Cleveland?
Repent of your sins
How do I repent Brother Cleveland?
250 Acknowledge your sins
Confess your sins and forsake them
Let the wicked forsake his way
An unrighteous man his thoughts
And let him come unto the Lord
255 And He'll have mercy upon him
And will verily pardon him
My God
If the people that's powerful
Would proffer themselves
260 And pray
And seek My faith
And turn from their wicked ways
Then they will hear from Him
[*unclear*]
265 The Scriptures say
Ain't willing to give up
Ain't willing to give up the LSD
Ain't willing to give up the marijuana
Ain't willing to give up they hatred
270 Ain't willing to give up they strife
Ain't willing to give up they cars
Put yourself in the right hand of God
And He will raise you up
God resents the powerful and gives grace to the humble
275 Bow your heads now where you are now

BISHOP E. E. CLEVELAND
SERMON 2
"He Wants Your Life: The Search for the Religion of Christ"

1 Everybody say Amen
Everybody say Amen
Thank God for another opportunity to be home again

Thank God for another opportunity to be here to bring you
   another message from the Lord
5 Thank God for the opportunity to preach on the search for the
   religion of Christ
   It's a blessed thing to be able to preach the Gospel in a time
   like this
   Men looking for something everywhere
   The world is in search for something and it don't know what they
   looking for
   But we found it
10 And it's all in Jesus
   He said without any doubt or disputation
   "Come to Me
   All ye that labor and are heavy laden and I'll give you rest"
   This old world is laboring
15 Laboring
   Laboring night and day
   People can't rest and sleep
   Troubled and confused and perplexed
   Torn, aggravated and agitated
20 Filled with anger and hate
   And filled with lust and pride and greed
   Filled with haughtiness and covetness
   Filled with doubts and fears
   Why? Because they missed the mark
25 They missed the boat
   They lost coming out of the deep end
   They didn't make it
   Jesus said here
   Listen to what He said
30 "Why call Me Lord, Lord
   And do not the things I say?"
   Everybody repeat after me
   Say it
   With your life
35 God is studying your tongue
   God is studying your aspirations
   God ain't studying your manipulations
   God ain't studying your demonstrations
   God ain't studying your words and your wisdom
40 God don't want your delay
   God wants your life

He said, "Come to Me."
If you're a fool come on
I'll give you some sense if you'll give Me your life
45   He's made unto us wisdom
My God, He said "Come to Me"
Thank God
If you're poor
He said, "I'm rich
50   And you'll be made rich through my poverty"
The world is mine
The fullness thereof and all that dwell therein
[unclear]
Come to Me if you're confused
55   I'll give you peace
Great peace have they who love God's law
And nothing shall offend them
He said, "Come to Me
Give Me your life
60   And I'll make your habitation a peaceful habitation"
Say Amen
Jesus wants your speech
And your life to balance
Get going
65   Ain't studying about you
If you say it with your lips
Demonstrate with your life
"Why call ye Me Lord and Master
And won't do the thing I tell you?"
70   He wants your life
He wants your motive
He wants your intention
He wants your purpose
He wants your objective
75   Say it with your life
Oh everybody tonight who calls himself a Christian
Dedicate your lives to God
Man we'll have this thing cleaned up
Before twenty-four hours
80   My God enough folk claiming religion
Claiming God
If they had it with their life
Like they had it with their dancing

Their shouting
85 They preaching
With they moaning
With their prayer
And with their testimony
If they had it with their lives
90 We'd turn this old world upside down
Thank God
Hallelujah to God
But you ain't got it
The world knows it and the church knows it
95 More folk going to church now than ever in the history of
      the world
Churches everywhere
Churches in the basements
Churches on the street corner
Churches in the storefronts and in the garages
100 Churches in the dwelling house and
Churches in the synagogues
Churches everywhere
Churches on the air twenty-four hours a day
Turn on the air and you'll hear somebody preaching church
105 Preaching, confessing and not possessing
Where's your life?
He wants your life
And not only does He want your life
Praise God
110 The balance, He wants your life of prayer
He said, Jesus said to Himself
"Men ought to always pray"
How many of us always pray?
How many of us live in a prayerful mood all the time?
115 We say, well I got to work and I can't be hooping and hollering up
      and down the streets
Folks have called me a neurotic, have called me a fool
Have called me a delusion
And a screwball
And off the deep end
120 But the Lord said you don't have to be that
You can always pray
Because prayer is the sense out of the heart
What is uttered or expressed

Hallelujah to God
125 You can pray and don't have to utter a word
Thank God
He knows your thoughts are far off
And He knows your pride and your doubts in Him
He knows all of your ways
130 Not a word in your tongue
And he knows it all together
Don't you know He wants your life?
Man don't need no wife to tell him she loves him and won't do
   nothing he tell her to do
He wants our lives
135 I want you to do what I say
Don't want you to go when you say go
I want you to go when I say go
I want you to come when I say come
I want you to be where I want you to be
140 Whatever I want you to do
I want you to do
You belong to me
Your life is mine
If you're going to be my wife
145 You gotta do what I say do
Give up your life to your mother, your grandmother
Give up your life of your buddies, your friends
And if I say do a thing
I don't care who say don't do it
150 Do what I do
As old Jesus say
"If you love Me, keep My word"
If you love Me and don't keep your word, I say you're a liar and the
   truth's not in you
My God, if God done turn this world over
155 Every man in here done hypocrite if you don't think with God
You done fooled around and lost out with God
And now God done turned the whole thing over to fakes and
   phonies
Nobody can't believe nothing hardly nobody says
Everybody's a front and a put-on and a put-up
160 A make-up and a make-out
White-washed and not washed white
Glory to God

And nobody have no confidence in nobody
He say, "I want your life"
165   Not only do He want your life in prayer
He wants your life
My God
In obedience
He say "Follow Me"
170   And you can't follow nobody unless you go wherever they go
Follow Me
My God
And you know He did no sin
And there was no downfall in His mouth
175   You know
My God
The folks that crucified Him
And the folks
My God
180   That condemned Him
Had to close out by saying
"Master, you told the truth
Last time they had you on Calvary"
Surely, this man must be the son of God
185   Hallelujah to God
He wants your life
That's what He wants
He wants your consecration
He wants your life
190   My God
And He looks at the life that will pay
And make a contribution
[*unclear*]
When He was giving
195   The Bible say
He moved on over beside the table to see what they were giving
Don't make no difference how much you give
It's how you give
If you give with all you got
200   Then it don't make no difference if it ain't but a penny
If you giving with all you got
Put all you got in it
[*unclear*]
Jesus say, "He give Me more than all of you"

205 Thank God
And he wants lives
He wants lives that will obey
He wants lives that will be dedicated
He wants lives that will be consecrated
210 He wants lives to be sacrificed
Thank God
He that come to Me
My God
Nothing but the mother and father of his own children
215 Or even his own flesh
[unclear]
My God, He say
You come to Me
Thank God
220 If you don't tell Him everything
You just keep everything
Rich young ruler came to Him and said
Master, what good thing can I do
What might I give to the Almighty
225 To enter the Kingdom of God
He said
Give Me your life
You shall not steal
You shall not commit adultery
230 You shall not bear false witness
You shall not covet
And drink Jesus
He thought he would do these things
He said
235 Good things for me Master
All these things you said I had to do
I done it from my youth
He said, wait
One more thing you got to do
240 Go out and sell what you got
Give it to the poor
And come on and follow Me
I want your life
Thank God
245 I want everything you got
And if you don't give Him everything

You can keep everything
Hallelujah to God
Amen
250 I heard somebody say
I surrender Lord
I surrender all to Thee my Blessed Savior
I surrender Lord
And He wants your everything
255 He wants you to come as you say
Just as I am
Without one plea
But that your blood
Was shed for me
260 If you bid me come to Thee
Oh Lamb of God I come
I come
He wants lives
My God
265 Any man that's dedicated
He wants lives
My God
That will pray and obey
He wants lives that will yield
270 Is your heart on the altar
Of sacrifice laid?
Your heart does the Spirit control
You can only be blessed
You have sleep and sweet rest
275 When you yield Him
Your body and your soul
Thank God
He's tired of folk who are saying and ain't doing
He said
280 "Listen, with your mouth you confess Me
But with your hearts you move far from Me"
Ain't how you testify
But how'd you live last week
How did you live?
285 That's what He's talking about
You didn't live nothing
You ain't done nothing
He ain't gonna pay you for putting on

But He's gonna pay you for really living
290 Said in Matthew 16:24
He said
He wants you to follow Him in consecration
How many lives is consecrated to God tonight?
Come in and love Him
295 He that seeks of your joy
How many folks love Him
Better than you love anything else in the world?
He said, If you love Me
Amen
300 Keep My word
He said
If you love Me feed My sheep
If you love Me feed My lamb
He wants you to know
305 That you got to put up or shut up
If you say you love Him
You got to do something about it
We got plenty churches
We got plenty preachers
310 We ain't got many folks who have given their lives to Jesus Christ
I don't care what nobody thinks about Him
The dope fiend has given up his life
For dope
He's given up his life for dope
315 And everybody's signed him over as a dope fiend
Nobody expect nothing out of him
But just another shot in the veins
The liquor head has given his life for liquor
And everybody expects him to be drunk everyday
320 And he gets drunk and stays that way
Getting on the plane this evening in Los Angeles
To come up here
And they packed and jammed that great big old seven-o-seven
It was packed and jammed
325 And there was two fellas come out with me
And was coming and was way back in the line
And says
I say look all those folks gonna get on this plane
I say can you imagine
330 All these folks gonna get up in the air

Swinging with nothing under them?
And one of the fellas said to me
Said, are you a preacher?
I said, yes
335 He said, how you know you was called to preach?
I said, how I know I was called
I say, the way I know I was called
The Bible said that God out of Jesus
And that Bible said that He endowed Him with the Holy Ghost
and with power
340 Who went about doing good and healing all that was oppressed by
the Devil
I said, listen, have you known folks to be given up to murder until
they would kill a man?
You can tell they been drinking
[*unclear*]
[*unclear*]
345 [*unclear*] prayer on the plane
346 Come let us pray now

REV. CARL J. ANDERSON
SERMON 1
"In Times Like These"

1 If you have your Bible
You will find one in the back of the pew
You may turn with me to the sixth chapter of our Lord's
Gospel according to St. John and we're going to read the
5 Sixty-sixth to the sixty-ninth verses where you will find the
words of
The text. St. John chapter six verses sixty-six through sixty-ninth
"From that time, many of His disciples went back and walked no
more
With Him. Then said Jesus unto the Twelve, will ye also go away?
Then Simon Peter answered Him 'Lord, to whom shall we go?
10 Thou has the words of eternal life and we believe and are sure
That Thou art that Christ, the Son of the Living God.'"
I shall use as my theme tonight
Seeing the condition of the world
The people that is in it
15 My theme is
In Times Like These

In Times Like These
You understand it
I have been somewhat busy today
20 We have been blessed by the visitation of the Holy Spirit
Just about everybody is wondering about times like these
And those of you here and in radioland that are listening in
I'm sure that you can look at the conditions now and say we're
Seeing things, hearing things, that we have never seen or heard
25 Before. But to you who are Bible readers who study the word
    of the
Lord and know that these are the signs of the coming of our Lord
From the Scriptures read and others that will be read or
    quoted later
We shall speak to you from the theme "In Times Like These"
Children, when we think rightly about our past you know
30 We know that it is our assigned duty and our faithfulness is
The performance of our assigned duty. But first we would
Like to rightly appraise our times.
Help me Lord Jesus
What's wrong with our times?
35 What's good or bad in times like these?
What's good children
Or what is bad?
These are times of great excitement
And I'm sure you'll agree with me
40 But did you know that out of all of this
Happening around us
There are many so-called Christians
Who are yet asleep?
Spiritually asleep
45 My, my, my
These great excitements
Kidnapping
Unusual murders
Robbery
50 War threats
Am I right?
World Series
And hundreds of other things keep up excitement around
    the clock
Help me Lord Jesus
55 These are times of great excitement

Yes sir
We have more good schools than any other country on earth
And also more crime than other countries
Lord have mercy
60   These are times of more crime than any other time
People are now afraid to walk the streets
But let me remind you of the word of God
This is just the beginning of sorrow
Yes sir
65   And now if these is the beginning of sorrow
Then that Christian should draw closer to Lord Jesus
Am I right about it
The great amusements
We have bowling
70   Baseball
Basketball
Boxing
Dog races
Foot races
75   Horse shows
Style shows
Leg shows
And please see the daily papers for others
These are times of great unrest
80   From top to the bottom
Of our society
We have airships
And battleships
And almost every other kind except
85   Fellowship
Help me Holy Spirit
And this fellowship that gives peace
Unnhnnn
Of mind, good will toward men
90   These are times my good sisters and brothers
Of great recreational programs
In and out of the church
Many people are dying without being regenerated
And born in the Spirit of God
95   Lord have mercy
These are times when many are turning back
Into the world of sin

Oh, the countless Christians that are going back into the
    wilderness
Some are fading, and some are doubting
100 These are times of spiritual darkness
Of moral weakness
Millions of church members on the fence of indecision
Trying to run with the hare and 'ho with the hound
These are times when the words of Jesus are being fulfilled
105 Even in our day
Isn't that right
We're finding false teachers
False prophets
Arising everyday
110 And deceiving many
Help me Lord Jesus
People are running to all kinds of religions now
To anything that's new
You have a crowd that's running there
115 Help me Holy Spirit
These are times when men have itching ears to hear
    something new
But refuse to obey the teaching of the old or the new
These are times of recession on the spiritual front
Lord help me please
120 Membership is often accepted for Christianity
And reputation is pawned off for character
These are times
When men, women, boys and girls
Are in a hurry doing nothing
125 And going nowhere
Help me Holy Spirit
And some way they are going is to an early grave
Yes sir
And big times
130 And big schools
Big religious organizations
Guide me Holy Spirit
I'll hook this train up in a minute
We delight in talking about our thousands of members and billions
    of dollars in property and money
135 Yes my children
These are times of great external improvements

And internal decay
When most of our churches are ice cold
I know I'm right about it
140   You don't find an amen corner too live now
As Jesus puts it
"With your lips you serve Me
But your heart is far from Me"
Help me Lord
145   But I'm always saying
Lord, deliver me from a dead church
Times of great days in our streamlined churches
Children's day
Men's day
150   Women's day
Rally day
Father's Day
Mother's Day
Homecoming day
155   And a flock of other days
But the Day of Pentecost is never experienced
Help me Lord Jesus
Guide me Lord
If anyone cries Amen in the church today
160   The old hypocrite look around and wonders what's wrong with him
When the Lord say make a joyful noise
Come to the Lord
Am I right about it
Christ is crowded out
165   We've crowded the Lord out of the picture
For there is no room for him now
Yes sir
Now that we have briefed you on times like these
Since we have many manmade things
170   Rolling into the world
Under the guise of Christian religion
The question arises
What is Christian religion
Lord, have mercy
175   Did you know the sinner man and the sinner woman is
          standing on
The outside
Looking at the so-called Christians doing the things of the world

Guide me Holy Spirit
Religion means any system, faith and worship but this is
180   Not the meaning of Christian religion
There are many manmade religions
But the wisest man that ever been born
The best man that ever lived
And the most faithful to testify
185   Could not produce the Christian religion in a million years
Guide me Holy Spirit
The Christian religion is the free religion
And I'm glad salvation is free
Aren't you glad about it
190   Guide me Holy Spirit
Yeah
I'm glad that often parents pray for their children
To accept Jesus
But this is far as they go
195   'Cause the matter of accepting Jesus and the religion
Is for the individual to decide
"He that believeth and is baptised
Shall be saved"
Can I get a witness?
200   Guide me Holy Spirit
Yeah and not only that
The Christian religion is the only religion that Jesus authorized
Yeah, "If thou stand empowered ye shall have power"
It's the heaven sent soul-filling religion
205   It's the working out of the in-dwelling of the spirit
Working within the will of God
Christian religion is the only pure religion
Its mission is to motivate
Accelerate and
210   Integrate
Elevate and purify
Every believer in Christ
I know I'm right about it
Yeah
215   So many people in the world
Got this business turned around
Yeah
And every Christian religion is like Christ
The author and the finisher

220 The same yesterday
     Today and forever
     Yeah
     It comes not so much from what we know
     As it does from what we believe
225 Have I got a witness?
     It comes not so much from teaching
     As it does from preaching
     Yeah, some love singing more than they love the Gospel
     Let me tell you the Gospel is the only thing that will save your
230 Dying soul
     Oh yes
232 For the Gospel is power

REV. CARL J. ANDERSON
SERMON 2
"Ezekiel and the Vision of Dry Bones"

  1 If you have your Bibles ready
     You may turn with me
     To the thirty-seventh chapters of the book of Ezekiel
     And we're going to read
  5 The first, second and third verse
     "The hand of the Lord
     Was upon me
     And carried me out in the Spirit of the Lord
     And set me down
 10 In the midst of the valley which was full of bones"
     You understand that
     "And cause me to pass by them round about
     And behold there was very many in the open valley
     And lo, they were very dry"
 15 You understand me
     I want to use as my theme tonight
     Ezekiel and the Vision of Dry Bones
     You understand
     Not dry bones in the valley
 20 But Ezekiel and the Vision of Dry Bones
     And this is one message from the Lord that you cannot run away
         from it
     Yes sir
     He that is led by the Spirit

They are the sons of God
25 And I feel sorry for that individual
That only loves sin
And runs from the Gospel
For it will take the Gospel to save your soul
Now this new Ezekiel signifies God's way of thinking
30 Ezekiel is known as one of the most mysterious Hebrew prophets
Yes sir
And he began, well, as a boy
He grew up under the influence of Jeremiah
And he began to prophesy at the age of thirty
35 And for twenty-two years preached by the River of Shafar
At Talabinth
And history says he died at the age of fifty-two
Now this man Ezekiel styles himself
The son of man
40 Several times he uses this expression
"Thus sayeth the Lord"
You understand me
And you'll find one hundred and seventeen times
Yes sir
45 The times of his prophesy was stormy and traditional
Ezekiel had two audiences
One real and present, the exiled about him
And the other the whole house of Israel
You understand me
50 Yes sir
And you'll find many dry Christians in church
As I oftentimes say
I wouldn't have a religion I can't feel
Ezekiel used allegories or parables such as those of Israel as a
founding child
55 Representing one with a sound body but unable to walk
Do you understand me
And second as a lioness
Third a stately figure
And fourth a vine doomed
60 Yes sir
He employed symbolic actions depicting the siege of Jerusalem
By dividing his hair into three parts
Do you understand me
First part to be burned

65 Second part to be smitten
    And the third part to be scattered representing
    Do you understand me
    Israel and Jerusalem when one-third of the city was smitten
    With the sword and the gates were set on fire
70 Help me Lord
    Another third representing the scattered Jews all over the world
        today
    Now by way of parenthesis
    I sometimes wonder why
    The Lord chose that the hair from Ezekiel's head would be divided
        three times
75 Yes sir
    And then as I began to search
    I find that one is Heaven's unity number
    And seven is Heaven's sacred number
    You understand me
80 But three is Heaven's complete number
    Whatever God does He does completely
    Am I right about it
    I want the world to know
    That there are three Heavenly bodies
85 Yes sir
    The sun
    Moon
    And the planets
    Guide me Lord
90 The earth is constituted of three great elements
    They are land, water and air
    And these have three different forms
    You understand me
    And they are solid, liquid and vapor
95 Help me Holy Spirit
    Yes sir
    Three kinds of animal life
    Animals that inhabit the earth
    Fish inhabit the waters
100 And fowls the air
    Am I right about it?
    Well, I turn to the Bible
    And I read where Noah had three sons
    Sham, Ham and Jephtha

105   Yes sir
       You know it's difficult
       To preach to people who do not read their Bible
       Yes sir
       And I read where Moses was hidden for three months
110   Can I get a witness?
       Yeah, his life was divided into three periods
       Forty years in Pharaoh's house
       Forty years in the wilderness
       And forty years in leadership
115   You understand me
       And the workmen of Solomon's temple
       Were divided into three classes
       Seventy thousand entered apprentices
       Eighty thousand fellow craftsmen
120   And three thousand six hundred master masons
       Help me Holy Spirit
       And not only that, Daniel prayed three times a day
       Yes sir
       So you see three is important   *
125   The Hebrew children
       Shadrack, Meshack and Abednego
       Composed Heaven's fireproof unit
       Yes sir
       And when Jesus was born
130   Three wise men came from the East
       And presented three kinds of gifts
       Am I right about it?
       When the Master wanted to confirm his divine nature
       And mission in the minds of disciples
135   He took three of them
       Peter, James and John
       Am I right about it
       Yeah, and He took them into a high mountain
       Apart and was transfigured before them
140   And Peter got happy there
       And said
       Let us build three tabernacles
       Am I right about it?
       Yes sir
145   One for Thee
       One for Moses

And one for Elijah
So the Lord told Ezekiel to divide his hair
After having shaved his head with a barber's razor
150   In three parts
Ezekiel used other symbols
He stood out on the street and ate bread with feminine hands
Representing the failing of the stall of life
He set his furniture out of his house
155   In the broad daylight
Representing the holy vessels and the furniture of the temple
Would be moved out before their eyes
Not only did he speak by parables and symbols
But he saw, he saw visions of the glory of God
160   Am I right about it?
Yes sir
Of the restored sanctuary and of our discourse this evening
Of the valley of dry bones
My brothers and sisters
165   In the Lord there are many valleys
Am I right about it?
Now the children of Israel were pictured as in bondage
While in Babylon, Ezekiel was with them in servitude
He heard their cry as is recorded in the one hundred thirty-
          seventh number of the Psalms
170   Judah had lost her political existence as a nation
And their temple was destroyed
And the beautiful service of Jehovah was abolished
I'll hook this train up in a minute
And the walls of Jerusalem was torn down
175   And the gates had been set on fire
All because the nations had been unfaithful to God
And prepared that their very name was going to be wiped out
From the remembrance of God
In their sorrow they cried
180   Our bones are dry
You understand me
Our hopes is lost
And we are cut off from our parts
They looked upon themselves, children
185   As dead in the sight of God
You know it's a bad thing to walk around with the name Christian
          and do not have no spirit

Am I right about it?
They would find that they resemble the body in the grave
Which nothing remains
190 And I see Ezekiel he was true to his calling
Yes sir
And he was wearied over the plight of Judah
And the Lord set him down in the valley that was full of bones
Yeah, he saw
195 You understand me
He saw the flesh
Had been devoured
So to speak
By animals and vultures
200 He saw bones had been bleached by the chilly winds and
          parching sun
Yeah, he saw bones scattered by the rolling chariots and the
          clattering of the horses
And these bones were dry
Do you understand me
They were so dry no footsteps could be heard anywhere
205 Yeah, it's a sad thing
Yeah, to go to church and find Christians all dry
Yeah, and when the Lord said
Yes sir, when the Lord said make a joyful noise
Am I right about it?
210 Make it unto the Lord all ye lambs
And right now the world is making their noise
The nightclubs are dancing by the tune of the band
Yeah, and the blues and rock and roll singers
Yeah, those who set around are clapping their hands and they're
          saying to their favorite singer "Come on!"
215 You understand me
And I think that you shouldn't mind me crying about Jesus
Yeah, I want to make a noise about the Lord Jesus Christ
I'm so glad
That I'm able to make a noise
220 And He's been so good to me
Yeah, has He been good to you
Somebody said that the Lord was so good to them
But they never make any noise about what the Lord has said
A woman met Jesus down at the well
225 You understand me

And He told her everything that she had done
She dropped the water pot and ran downtown saying
"Come and see a man that told me all that I did!"
Oh Lord
230 Yeah, now this woman can tell what Jesus done for her
Yeah, I think the church ought to witness what the Lord has done
    for you
Yeah, early one morning
Yeah, I found the Lord
Yes I did
235 I was in the valley of dry bones
Yeah, I had no God on my side
Yeah, I didn't have no spirit
To make me shout
But when I found the Lord
240 I found joy
Yeah, joy
Yeah, joy was found
I found joy
244 Peace to my dying soul

HIS GRACE, KING LOUIS H. NARCISS
Untitled Sermon

1 Great is the Lord
And greatly to be praised
In the city of our God
Right here in the mountains of His holiness
5 For great is God
And greatly to be praised
We come this hour at the close of another evening
To thank God
For His great and many blessings
10 Each Sunday we talk to you
Endeavoring to express to you God
God in spirit
And God in truth
But because there are so many spirits here
15 And they're housed in various bodies
Each spirit tries to make its presentation
They ask Jesus this question
"To whom should we give honor to?"

But He being a spirit
20 He knew their craftiness
And from among them came a penny
And He asked them
"And whose inscription came upon this penny?"
And they said "Caesar"
25 And He said
"Give unto Caesar that which belongs to Caesar
And unto God, that which belongs to God"
I'm not satisfied with just my accomplishments alone
Or with my knowing that God is with me and that He is a spirit
30 And that He does work in me
And He is in this temple
But Jesus who also was confronted with this problem
He said unto them when they asked Him about the spirits
He said to them in the fifteenth chapter of St. John
35 "I am the true vine"
For they have heard about the vine
They had heard about the Messiah
Like unto you
They had heard the enchantment of thousands of voices
40 And voices of multitudes of people
Giving praise to God in their own way
But they never knew Him
They asked of Him
Are you Elijah
45 For they believed in Elijah
No
And some asked Him
They were trying to find out something
Are you Moses
50 And the older ones said "No"
He could not be Moses 'cause he's not yet
Forty years old
You see, he was very young
And they asked Him
55 Some took Him to be John the Baptist
And John said
He's coming after me
And I'm not worthy to unlace His sandals
I'm not worthy to touch Him
60 And this inquisition went on and on

Today people are asking this question
Though they shout
Though they say Amen
Though they praise God in their way
65   But yet they never knew the spirit
Among the holy ones He sought and couldn't find the answers
Caesar Augustus said well I'd rather not bother with him
Herod tried to kill Him
In the end
70   They couldn't kill Him
For the same spirit tried way back yonder in Moses' day
And God touched the heart of Moses' mother
And taught her how to weave a basket
And put him in the river called Nile
75   Well
The little homemade ark floated
Until Pharaoh the King's daughter's heart was pierced
People tonight have not yet realized or considered
What it means to be in someone's heart
80   So Jesus kept on searching
And He met a group of men called themselves fishermen
By trade or profession
And all night they had caught nothing
Have you caught anything in your life
85   I don't mean a hug or an embrace made of someone
I don't mean a fantastic lie
Or a mirror-proving lie
You know getting love in a mirror
Proving how you gonna talk, you know
90   But have you really caught the truth in your life
Or have you ever stopped to consider
So He said to these men
You're fishing how long
They said all day and all night
95   And we've caught nothing
He said "cast your net on the other side"
Oh, my friends you ought to change your sides tonight
You ought to cast your nets over on God's side
'Cause they caught nothing
100   Maybe all of your life your religion has meant nothing to you
Your faith is wonderful and beautiful until testing time comes
Can you stand the test

Can you prove that your faith can remove mountains
That mountain in your life
105 He saw in the midsts of these men
A man saw something
And He gathered them together and He asked them
Who am I?
I've asked this question said the Messiah
110 And no one answers
Whom do men say I am
And they went through their long ceremonies
And He wasn't interested in their ceremonies and their rituals
He said, Oh you Pharisees
115 Oh you Pharisees
Who are bound by your customs and your belief
Said but yet, you never knew Me
Peter said, "I know who you are"
Peter was not considered a holy man
120 He was touched
He said what came up came out
He said "but I know who you are"
Do you know Him tonight?
He said "Thou art the Christ
125 The Son of the Living God"
Never before had the universe received this annunciation
And never before had any man or woman received this salutation
And Jesus said unto him, "Peter!"
And I now speak from the sixteenth Book of St. Matthew
130 And the eighteenth verse
Peter, I'm gonna change you
For you spoke something that no man or woman knew
For the earth has never yielded this truth before
Said upon this rock
135 I will build
Not the temple for there is a difference in the temple
But the church
And the very gates of Hell
Shall not prevail again
140 A temple, the Bible said
Defile not your bodies
For they are the physical temples of God
And God will not dwell in an unclean temple
The Bible said and they build unto Him a temple

145 And everybody's not allowed to enter the old temple
        One must work his way into the temple
        Must know how to prove his own worth
        And properly identify himself
        But the church
150 But whosoever will, let him come
        And He said to them
        I'm gonna teach you a prayer
        And they asked Him
        Teach us a prayer to pray
155 And He said
        When you enter the secret closet
        Shut the door
        Seek the Father
        In the Spirit
160 And in the truth
        And He shall reward you openly
        And He asked them
        Let the words of my mouth
        Have you asked Him that, ever
165 In your life or are you waiting 'til trouble arises
        He asked them
        Let the meditation of my heart
        Be acceptable in your sight
        Will thou seek Me now
170 While in My veins and in your veins
        Run our own blood
        Seek Me while My own heart
        You ought to think about it
        Is beating in My own body
175 While I stand
        On My own feet
        By the strength of My own body
        As given to me by God
        And they said . . .
        [*King Narciss and the congregation sing "Let the Strength of Thy
           Body."*]
180 Oh yes
        And they said
        [*Congregation*:]   Our Father
        According to His teaching He is

<pre>
                              Our Father
185   Which art in Heaven
                              Hallowed be Thy name
        Well, thank you Jesus
                              Thy Kingdom come
                              Thy will be done
190   On earth
                              As it is
                              In heaven
        Give us this day our daily bread
                              Give us this day
195   Our daily bread
                              And forgive us our debts
                              As we forgive our debtors
                              And lead us not
                              Into temptation
200   But deliver us
                              From evil
                              For thine
                              Is the Kingdom
                              And the power
205   And the glory
                              Forever
                              Amen
        Hail Mary   Hail Mary
        Full of grace   Full of grace
210   The Lord is   The Lord is with thee
           with thee
        Blessed art   Blessed thou art among women
           thou women
        And blessed is   And blessed is the fruit
           the fruit
        Of thy womb,   Of thy womb, Jesus
           Jesus
        Holy Mary   Holy Mary
215   Mother of God   Mother of God
        Pray for us   Pray for us sinners
           sinners
        Now   Now
        And at the hour   And at the hour
        Of our death   Of our death
</pre>

220 Amen   Amen
    You know I feel Him and I'm glad about it
    You know that's my testimony
    Praise Him
    You know what I can't tell you in words
225 I tell you in a song
    That's my living testimony
    I came to Jesus as I was
    Very [unclear] and fast
    But I found something
230 I found in that same Jesus
    God gave me a resting place
    And it stopped the firelike burning
    Inside of me
    And it stopped the prayer wheel-like turning
235 Inside of me
    Oh yeah
    I don't mean just when I have a petition before Him
    I'm talking about after I got the answers from the petition
    Thank you Jesus
240 Thank you Jesus
    You know God wants to be praised
    Thank you Jesus
    After He crossed the Israelites across the Red Sea
    They got tired of praising Him
245 But you ought to look back from whence you came
    And think about what brought you over
    Thank you Jesus
    Yeah
    Yes
250 Think about Him
    Somebody say [unclear] isn't working for the Lord
    Tell me what will I do
    You see He's hungry
    I said He's hungry for somebody to praise Him
255 And those that used to praise Him don't praise Him no more
    Because they found the answer
    I said they don't praise Him no more
    Because they found the answer
    Yeah
260 But don't wait until sorrow or troubles come your way
    To cry out to Him

Or while the blood, your blood is running warm
In your veins
Come on out to the house of God
265 Come on out and take your time
[*Announcements*]
[*Unclear*]
You know it's wonderful
Amen
I hear so many times
270 Pastors of our radio church
You know we have some pastors of the church
And we have some pastors of the radio church
This is one that broadcasts
Amen
275 So many times your announcements don't get through
Because just about when you ready to give the address that you
   know so well
And we don't know
Somebody hollers Amen and that's right and we don't get it
And we be wishing sometimes that you go over it again
280 Amen
I heard Pastor Anderson of Golden Gate Baptist Church
Preaching this evening
And he said something
And the folks said Amen
285 And they were enjoying theyself
And he said I'm gonna say it again
And he took his time and said it again
[*Unclear*]
[*Unclear*] and I said to you thank you
290 I'd like to take some time to take some of my radio time
And help somebody
For I feel
That it is expedient
And essential
295 That we teach you how to live in this world
Do you know the reasons many aren't making it is because they
   don't know how
Years will pass
Minutes will make hours
Hours will make days
300 And days will make weeks

And weeks will keep on passing will make a month
And twelve months will make a year
And you'll find yourself eighteen years old, twenty-one, thirty-
   five, forty, fifty
Sixty, seventy or eighty
305 And never grown up
Because you stopped growing
Number one, there are grown men and women
Who have never been taught
I thought of an incident someone said to me one day
310 Meaning no harm
Said, did something for me and I enjoyed it and said thank you
And he said thank you for what
Well, I think the world needs to know about that
Have you ever saw a sign in a store that said thank you for your
   patronage
315 [*Unclear*]
Now Job learned this
He said in the thirty-second chapter and ninth verse of this book
Great men are not always wise
And neither does old have men good understanding or judgment
320 Because you have a great position my friends
This does not make you know what to do
Sometimes you can run from a gnat
You know the little bug get in your eye
And run into a herd of buffalo
325 And turn from them into a stampede of elephants
And you know they can mangle you far more than the gnat
Black man
Black woman
You gonna live and make your society learn to respect your ability
330 Organization, system, God, appreciation and say Thank you
For God is a god of love and He hates no one
But a liar
God hates a liar
My friend as we arriving in His day
335 Think about what I am saying
Value your power structure
And pay heed to your ways
And do good while you can
And let me bring it on down home to you
340 I heard on the radio today, a church went off this evening

And I asked one of the brothers
What's that church on the radio just now
I heard some pop singing you know
And he looked at me and laughed and said ain't no church now
345 And they were jumping
And so I let 'em jump on out
So after awhile I said, I thought they had some colored, you know
Churches on there
That's what you would say too
350 And after awhile I heard someone say
"What He done for other . . ."
I say, Oh there they come
Now the first thing they want to tell Him is what they did for the
    other fella
Come do it for me
355 I say, you think God gonna do for me what He did for these other
    fellas
No
You think God gonna do for you what he did for Mr. Rockefeller,
    Mr. Kennedy, Mrs. Kennedy
You know what He gonna do for you
And they laughed
360 I say He gonna give you some chitlins.
361 [*Unclear beyond this point*]

Notes

PREFACE

1. Paul Carter Harrison, *Kuntu Drama: Plays of the African Continuum* (New York: Grove Press, 1974), 12–13.

INTRODUCTION

1. Hans A. Baer, *The Black Spiritual Movement: A Religious Response to Racism* (Knoxville: The University of Tennessee Press, 1984), 29.
2. At one point in a sermon preached on February 11, 1981, Cleveland said of himself that he had "been a preacher for over fifty-five years, and preaching the same old cornfield doctrine" (254). In the next several lines, however, he shares some very contemporary thinking on the advantages of natural foods over those assisted by synthetic additives. In many ways, Cleveland is very much a contemporary thinker.
3. Virgilius Ferm, ed., *Encyclopedia of Religion* (New York: Philosophical Library, 1945), 291.
4. Quotation from *Encyclopedia of Religion*, 340.
5. Kenneth Pike, *Language in Relation to a Unified Theory of the Structure of Human Behavior*, pt. 1 (Glendale: Summer Institute of Linguistics, 1954), 10, 93; Alan Dundes, "From Etic to Emic Units in the Structural Study of Folktales," *Journal of American Folklore* 75 (April/June 1962): 95–105.
6. Ibid., 96.
7. Ibid., 101.
8. J. Gordon Melton, ed., and James V. Geiger, *A Directory of Religious Bodies in the United States* (New York: Garland, 1977), 235–79. African-American colleagues Ernest Dunn and the late Vera Green have vigorously challenged my conceptualization of certain churches as being "more" African-American or Black than others. Particularly, they make reference to a large number of congregations which have been administratively and theologically affiliated with European denominations but which have historically had all-Black congregations. My response continues to be based on the way persons in those congregations perceive themselves. Until very recently, a Black member of an Episcopalian congregation or a Quaker Meeting, for instance, would consider himself or herself "Episcopalian" or "Quaker" first. I contend that this is a holdover from those years when upwardly mobile Blacks would eschew anything "black" in favor of quasi-European associations. Members of Black affective or charismatic congregations tend to perceive themselves in non-

European images and vaguely, if uncomfortably, perceive their historical origins as African-derived.

9. KDIA, with offices and studios in Oakland, Calif., serves the San Francisco–Oakland–Berkeley–San Jose listening area. Originally programmed to serve the Bay Area African-American population, the station has recently changed its format to a disco orientation and has developed a following among non–African-Americans as well.

10. The May 1971 field trip to Johns Island, S.C., was supported by a grant from the Center for Urban Ethnography, University of Pennsylvania (NIMH Grant MH-17216); the January 1971 field trip to Johns Island was supported through the Department of English, University of Delaware at Newark, and was made possible by Dr. Kathryn Morgan to whose class of African-American students I served as fieldwork consultant.

11. John Hope Franklin, "The Past in the Future of the South," in *Continuity and Change in the South*, ed. Edgar Thompson (Durham: Duke University Press, 1965), 435–50.

12. Melvin D. Williams, *On the Street Where I Lived*, Case Studies in Cultural Anthropology (New York: Holt, Rinehart and Winston, 1981), 122–24.

13. Ibid.; Williams's excellent ethnographies of two African-American communities in Pittsburgh could as easily apply to communities throughout the U.S. South.

14. John Blassingame, *The Slave Community: Plantation Life in the Antebellum South* (New York: Oxford University Press, 1972), 61. In a footnote to her article "Talking Trash in the Okefenoke Swamp Rim, Georgia," *Journal of American Folklore* 87 (October/November 1974), 340, Kay Cothran offers several positive references to "cracker culture." As used by most African-Americans, however, the term is derogatory and usually refers to unschooled, rural, openly bigoted white Americans, most frequently white southerners. "Nigger" is used here to mean a person who has mastered both the affect and deep meaning of African-American existence; a term of intense group identification. The term is also used derogatorily by large numbers of white Americans to apply to African-Americans and by African-Americans to suggest unsophistication.

In chaps. 2 and 3 of *The Mind of the Negro Reflected in Letters Written during the Crisis, 1800–1860* (Washington, D.C.: Association for the Study of Negro Life and History, 1926), Carter G. Woodson notes that African-Americans bought slaves in Louisiana, especially, not to imitate white plantation owners, but rather to "free" relatives who were then employed on plantations owned by the African-Americans. See also Woodson's monograph *The Education of the Negro Prior to 1861* (Washington, D.C.: Associated Publishers, 1915), and his book *A Century of Negro Migration* (Washington, D.C.: Association for the Study of Negro Life and History, 1918).

15. Blassingame, *Slave Community*; Don Yoder, *Pennsylvania Spirituals* (Hatboro: Folklore Associates, 1961); Bruce A. Rosenberg, "The Genre of the Folk Sermon," *Genre* 4 (June 1971): 189.

16. E. Franklin Frazier, *The Negro Church in America* (New York: Schocken, 1964), 1.

17. As used in this study, "style" is intended to mean a characteristic narrative modal event.

18. Walton Johnson, *Worship and Freedom: A Black American Church in Zambia* (New York: Africana Publishing Co., 1977).

19. *The Performed Word*, produced by Gerald L. Davis (Red Taurus Films), with a media grant from the National Endowment for the Humanities (PN-20146-81-0379) and under the sponsorship of the Anthropology Film Center Foundation, Santa Fe, is a one hour ethnodocumentary film (also available in videotape), being distributed by the Center for Southern Folklore, Memphis, Tenn., and the Anthropology Film Center, Santa Fe, N.M.

CHAPTER 1: FINDING THE WHEAT IN THE CHAFF

1. Author interview with Mrs. Sylvia Guiton, May 1981.

2. Line 6 in Cleveland's "You're Just Not Ready" sermon.

3. William Labov and Joshua Waletzky, "Narrative Analysis: Oral Versions of Personal Experience," in *Essays on the Verbal and Visual Arts*, Proceedings of the annual Spring meeting of the American Ethnological Society, 1966, ed. June Helm (Seattle: University of Washington Press, 1966).

4. Daniel J. Crowley, *I Could Talk Old-Story Good: Creativity in Bahamian Folklore* (Berkeley/Los Angeles: University of California Press, 1966), 16; Bruce A. Rosenberg, "The Formulaic Quality of Spontaneous Sermons," *Journal of American Folklore* 83 (January/March 1970): 6; Roger D. Abrahams, "Patterns of Performance in the West Indies," in *Afro-American Anthropology: Contemporary Perspectives*, ed. Norman Whitten, Jr., and John F. Szwed (New York: Free Press, 1970).

5. Rosenberg, "Formulaic Quality," 6.

6. Henry H. Mitchell, *Black Preaching* (Philadelphia: Lippincott, 1970), 139.

7. Ibid., 163–64.

8. Robert Kellogg, "What Is an Oral Epic?" (paper presented at the Annual Meeting of the Modern Language Association, New York, December 27–30, 1976).

9. Albert Lord, *The Singer of Tales* (New York: Atheneum, 1965), 101.

10. Roger D. Abrahams, "Can You Dig It? Aspects of the African Esthetic in Afro-America" (paper presented at the African Folklore Institute, Indiana University, Bloomington, July 16–18, 1970), 14.

11. James Fernandez uses the phrase "narrowing circularity" in his article "Equatorial Excursions: The Folklore of Narcotic-inspired Visions in an African Religious Movement," in *African Folklore*, ed. Richard M. Dorson, to identify a dance movement among members of the Bwiti cult designed to diminish any sense of migratory progression among cult members.

12. Abrahams, "Can You Dig It?" 8.

13. George Kent, *Blackness and the Adventures of Western Culture* (Chicago: Third World Press, 1972), 17.

14. Gerald L. Davis, "Afro-American Coil Basketry in Charleston County, South Carolina: Affective Characteristics of an Artistic Craft in a Social Context," in *American Folklife*, ed. Don Yoder (Austin, University of Texas Press, 1976), 177.

15. Robert Plant Armstrong, *The Affecting Presence: An Essay in Humanistic Anthropology* (Urbana: University of Illinois Press, 1971), 3–4.

16. Alan Dundes, "The Devolutionary Premise in Folklore Theory," *Journal of the Folklore Institute* 6 (June 1969): 13.

17. Joe K. Fugate, *The Psychological Basis of Herder's Aesthetics* (The Hague: Mouton, 1966), 16.

18. Robert P. Armstrong, *The Affecting Presence*, 3, 4.

19. Stephen E. Henderson, *Understanding the New Black Poetry: Black Speech and Black Music as Poetic References* (New York: Morrow, 1973); Addison Gayle, Jr., *The Black Aesthetic* (New York: Doubleday 1971), and "Reclaiming the Southern Experience: The Black Aesthetic Ten Years Later," *Black World* 23 (September 1974): 20–29; Kent, *Blackness*, 17.

20. Robert P. Armstrong, *The Affecting Presence*, 3–4.

21. Richard Bauman, "Verbal Art as Performance," *American Anthropologist* 77 (June 1975): 290.

22. E. Franklin Frazier, *The Negro Church in America* (New York: Schocken, 1964), 17–19.

23. Dell H. Hymes, "The Ethnography of Speaking," *Readings in the Sociology of Language*, ed. Joshua A. Fishman (The Hague: Mouton, 1968), 119.

24. John Szwed's treatment of the sacred/secular or sacred/blues dichotomy in African-American cosmology in "Musical Adaptation among Afro-Americans," *Journal of American Folklore* 82 (April/June 1969): 112–31, is concise and comprehensive on aspects of the dichotomy; see also Charles Keil, *Urban Blues* (Chicago: University of Chicago Press, 1966), esp. 142–48.

25. Zora Neale Hurston, *The Sanctified Church* (Berkeley: Turtle Island Press, 1983), 83.

26. In "Can You Dig It?" Abrahams defines interlock in this manner: "The image of African performance which emerges here is of the community celebrating its sense of groupness by coordination of energies in the common creative enterprise, and doing so by taking binary oppositions, embodying them in a complexly integrated traditional form which utilizes these oppositions in the form of complementarities. This group focus is guaranteed through the practice of interlock, in which the distinction between performer and audience is made meaningless, for all perform to some degree. The good performers, then, differ from others in the community only in degree; they gain status not because of their virtuosity but for their ability to bring the community together in performance." Abrahams first brought the interlock/complementarity concept to my attention in a private communication in 1969. Then, and in the amplification cited above, Abrahams identifies a critical African-American performance principle, a principle which has proven to be elusive for many other students of African-American or African

diasporic performance. At one level, I respect the integrity of Abrahams's definition and speak of the concept as intended by Abrahams. Still, the concept has a deeper and more precise application to the exchange of features that commonly takes place across genre lines in African-American performance. It is this latter meaning of Abrahams's concept that is used most consistently in this study.

27. Brian Sutton-Smith, "Expressive Profile," *Journal of American Folklore* 84 (January/March 1971), 80–81.

28. Claude Lévi-Strauss, *The Raw and the Cooked* (New York: Harper and Row, Torchbooks, 1969); Alan Dundes, "Metafolklore and Oral Literary Criticism," *Monist* 50 (1966): 509.

29. Dan Ben-Amos, "Analytic Categories and Ethnic Genres," *Genre* 2 (September 1969): 286 (quotation), 275, 290–91.

30. William R. Bascom, "The Relationship of Yoruba Folklore to Divining," *Journal of American Folklore* 56 (April/June, 1943): 129–30, and *Ifa Divination: Communication between Gods and Men in West Africa* (Bloomington: Indiana University Press, 1969).

31. Maurice Merleau-Ponty, *The Primacy of Perception and Other Essays* (Evanston: Northwestern University Press, 1964), 182.

32. Melville J. Herskovits, *The Myth of the Negro Past* (New York: Harper, 1941), 227; William H. Pipes, *Say Amen, Brother! Old-time Negro Preaching: A Study in American Frustration* (New York: William-Frederick Press, 1951), 72; Crowley, *I Could Talk Old-Story Good*, 16.

33. Bruce A. Rosenberg, 30.

34. Lord, *The Singer of Tales*, 101; Rosenberg, "Formulaic Quality," 23.

35. Rosenberg, "Formulaic Quality," 25.

36. Bruce A. Rosenberg, "The Genre of the Folk Sermon," *Genre* 4 (June 1971): 189.

37. J. Mason Brewer, *The Word on the Brazos: Negro Preacher Tales from the Brazos Bottoms of Texas* (Austin: University of Texas Press, 1953); Bruce A. Rosenberg, *The Art of the American Folk Preacher* (New York: Oxford University Press, 1970); Mitchell, *Black Preaching*; Herskovits, *Myth*, chap. 7; Hortense Powdermaker, *After Freedom: A Cultural Study of the Deep South* (New York: Viking, 1939), chap. 4; Charles S. Johnson, *Shadow of the Plantation* (Chicago: University of Chicago Press, 1939), chap. 5; also by Johnson, *Growing Up in the Black Belt* (Washington, D.C.: American Council on Education, 1949), chap. 5; Frazier, *The Negro Church*; Benjamin E. Mays and Joseph W. Nicholson, *The Negro's Church* (New York: Institute of Social and Religious Research, 1933).

38. I am indebted to my friend and colleague Adrienne Lanier-Seward for her spirited insistence that I consult the Library of Congress holdings for additional, and excellent, listings of African-American sermons. The Special Negro Archives and Manuscripts Collections of Fisk University Library, Nashville, Tennessee, contain 22 catalogued items, including books, and approximately 250 uncatalogued sermons; the Springarn-Moorland Collections, Howard University, Washington, D.C., contain 141 catalogued items,

including books, and several hundred uncatalogued sermons; the Schomburg Collection of Negro Literature and History, New York Public Library, contains 103 catalogued items, including books, and about 350 uncatalogued sermons; the Negro Collection, Chicago Public Library (main branch), contains 44 catalogued items and no manuscripts. I suspect that when all of these collections are fully catalogued, the listings will increase dramatically.

39. Lawrence A. Davis, "The Negro Interpretation of the Bible," master's thesis, University of Kansas, 1941.

40. Crowley, *I Could Talk Old-Story Good*, 16.

41. Rosenberg, "Genre."

42. Elizabeth Kilham, "Sketches in Color: IV," *Putnam's Monthly* 15 (March 1870), p. 304.

43. Dundes, "The Devolutionary Premise," 14.

44. Rosenberg, "Formulaic Quality," 25.

45. James Watson, *Tales and Takings, Sketches and Incidents from the Itinerant and Educational Budget* (New York: Carlton and Porter, 1856), 151, 98.

46. Hymes, "Ethnography of Speaking," 119.

47. Ibid.; Alan Dundes, Introduction to the Second Edition of *Morphology of the Folktale*, by Vladimir Propp (Austin: University of Texas Press, 1968), xiii.

48. Milman Parry, "Studies in the Epic Technique of Oral Verse-Making I: Homer and Homeric Style," *Harvard Studies in Classical Philology* 41 (1930); Thomas W. Talley observes, "Thus Negro Folk Rhyme, with very few exceptions, are poetry where a music measure is the unit of measurement of the words rather than the poetic foot," (*Negro Folk Rhymes Wise and Otherwise, with a Study* [New York: Macmillan Co., 1922], 231).

49. Walter S. Ong, "World as View and World as Event," *American Anthropologist* 71 (1969), 636–40.

50. Lord, *The Singer of Tales*, 26.

51. The interlocking nature of African-American expressive systems across genre boundaries is identified by several authors. Abrahams, "Can You Dig It?" has already been cited; see also Szwed, "Musical Adaptation," 114–16, and Rosenberg, "Genre," 190, for further illustration.

Chapter 2: Oral Formula and the Performed African-American Sermon

1. Lord, *The Singer of Tales*.

2. Donald Frye, "The Present State of Oral Literary Studies in Old English" (paper presented at the annual meeting of the Modern Language Association, New York, December 1974), 2.

3. Rosenberg, "Formulaic Quality," 6.

4. Ibid., 21–22; Parry, "Studies in the Epic Technique of Oral Verse-Making I," 231.

5. Roger D. Abrahams, "Public Drama and Common Values in Two Carib-

bean Islands," *Trans-Action* (July/August 1968): 63–71; "The Training of the Man-of-Words in Talking Sweet," *Language and Society* 1, pp. 15–29; Roger D. Abrahams and Richard Bauman, "Sense and Nonsense on St. Vincent: Speech Behavior and Decorum in a Caribbean Community," *American Anthropologist* 73 (1971): 762–72.

6. Lord, *The Singer of Tales*, 26.

7. Rosenberg, "Formulaic Quality," 26.

8. Propp, *Morphology of the Folktale*, 19–65; Rosenberg, *Art*, 52.

9. Lord, *The Singer of Tales*, 37; see Labov and Waletzky, "Narrative Analysis," 12–44, esp. 21–30.

10. Mitchell, *Black Preaching*, 29.

11. Ibid.; Frazier, *The Negro Church*, 46.

12. Watson, *Tales and Takings*, 98.

13. Ibid.

14. Ibid.

15. Frazier, *The Negro Church*, 46.

CHAPTER 3: CHARACTERISTICS AND FUNCTIONS OF THE STRUCTURAL UNITS OF THE AFRICAN-AMERICAN SERMON

1. Labov and Waletzky, "Narrative Analysis," 22.

2. For a general, international distribution of the rabbit in folkloric materials, see Antti Aarne's *Verzeichnis der Märchentypen* (Helsinki: Folklore Fellows Communications, 1910). Stith Thompson translated and enlarged the Aarne index and published it as *Types of the Folk-tale* (Helsinki: Folklore Fellows Communications, 1928); see esp. category 1, Animal Tales. In Susan Feldman's *African Myths and Tales* (New York: Dell, 1963), there are two folktales involving rabbits or hares, one Bakongo and the other Thonga, pp. 141–56. For illustrations of the rabbit or hare in African-American folk materials, see Richard Dorson's *American Negro Folktales* (New York: Fawcett, 1967), esp. section 1, part 2, Animal and Bird Stories.

3. Crowley, *I Could Talk Old-Story Good*; Pipes, *Say Amen, Brother!*; Davis, "The Negro Interpretation."

4. Davis, "The Negro Interpretation"; Crowley, *I Could Talk Old-Story Good*; Pipes, *Say Amen, Brother!*; Mitchell, *Black Preaching*.

5. While there are some pastor congregations among the Society of Friends (Quakers), most regular gatherings, or Meetings, of the society are convened without benefit of a spiritual leader. Friends recognize the quality of "godliness" in every person and believe that God can and does speak through every person.

6. I am indebted to Dr. Oluyemi Kayode, criminologist on the faculty of the University of Ibadan, Nigeria, and Nigerian graduate students of Rutgers University for assistance in understanding the nature of proverb performance among Yoruba (Nigeria) men.

7. Rosenberg, "Formulaic Quality," 6.

8. Mitchell, *Black Preaching*, 139.

9. Martin Luther King, Jr.'s "I Have a Dream" sermon was delivered from the steps of the Lincoln Memorial in Washington, D.C., during the 1963 march on Washington.

10. In *Black Culture and Black Consciousness: Afro-American Folk Thought from Slavery to Freedom* (New York: Oxford University Press, 1977), Lawrence W. Levine quotes the following from an article written by J. Kennard, Jr., in 1845: "They condensed four or five (syllables) into one foot, or stretched out one to occupy the space that should have been filled with four or five; yet they never spoiled the tune. This elasticity of form is peculiar to the negro song." For a fuller discussion, see Kinnard's article "Who Are Our National Poets?" *Knickerbocker Magazine* 26 (1845), 338.

11. See Rosenberg, "Genre," p. 189, for "dramatic pause"; Labov and Waletzky, "Narrative Analysis," for "free-clause formula."

12. For an interesting discussion of the relationship between successful performance and the faculty of the "good mind" through which God's will is manifest in material culture performance, see Gregory Day's "Afro-Carolinian Art: Towards the History of a Southern Expressive Tradition," *Contemporary Art/Southeast* January/February 1978, pp. 10–21.

13. Abrahams, "Can You Dig It?" 8.

14. Brewer, *The Word on the Brazos*, 1, 2.

15. Frederich C. Tubach, "Exempla in the Decline," *Traditio* 18 (1962): 409; Paul Meyer, *Les contes moralises de Nicole Bozon* (Paris, 1889); Thomas F. Crane, *The Exempla, or Illustrative Stories from the Sermones Vulgares of Jacques de Vitry* (London, 1890); Laurits Boedker, *European Folktales* (Hatboro: Folklore Associates, 1963); J. Thomas Welter, *L'exemplum dans la literature religieuse et didactique du moyen âge* (Paris, 1927).

16. Boedker, *European Folktales*, 19.

17. Brewer, *The Word on the Brazos*, 2.

18. Gerhard Kuttner, "Wesen und Formen der deutschen Schwankliteratur des 15. Jahrhunderts," *Germanistische Studien* 52 (1934).

19. See Szwed's "Musical Adaptation," 112–21, and Paul Oliver's *Conversation with the Blues* (New York: Horizon Press, 1965).

20. Kent, *Blackness*.

21. See Labov and Waletzky, "Narrative Analysis," 32, 33–39.

22. Ibid., 21.

23. Roger D. Abrahams, *Deep Down in the Jungle: Negro Narrative Folklore from the Streets of Philadelphia*, 1st rev. ed. (Chicago: Aldine, 1970), 58–59; Howard W. Odum and Guy B. Johnson, *The Negro and His Songs* (Chapel Hill: University of North Carolina Press, 1925), 279–86.

24. Abrahams, *Deep Down in the Jungle*, 58–59.

25. Labov and Waletzky, "Narrative Analysis," 32.

26. Ibid.

27. Ibid., 37.

28. See Edward Sapir, "Sound Patterns in Language," *Language* 1 (1925): 56.

29. Walter S. Ong, "World as View and World as Event," *American Anthropologist* 71 (1969): 637–40; see also Sapir, "Sound Patterns," 37–51.
30. Rosenberg, "Genre," 193; Davis, "The Negro Interpretation," 1; Crowley, *I Could Talk Old-Story Good*, 16.
31. See William Bascom's article on "Verbal Arts," *Journal of American Folklore* 68 (April/June 1955): 245–52.
32. Ong, "World as View," 639.
33. David Strauss, "Music: A Physical Approach," *Pennsylvania Triangle* 57 (October 1969): 17–21.
34. Daniel Goode is associate professor of music in the Department of Music at Rutgers University; Goode is active in New York and national contemporary music circles and recently made his Carnegie Hall debut.
35. The Kay Sonagram is manufactured by Kay Elemetrics Company, Pine Brook, N.J. I am indebted to Donald Caccamise of the Economic Zoology Laboratory of Cook College, Rutgers University, and to his assistant, Peter Alexandro, for their patience and interest in this area of my research.
36. Mitchell, *Black Preaching*, 163–64.
37. Armstrong, 3–4.

CHAPTER 4: THE TESTING OF THE PERFORMED AFRICAN-AMERICAN SERMON MODEL

1. Szwed, "Musical Adaptation," 219–27; Bennett quotation from *The Negro Mood and Other Essays* (Chicago: Johnson Publishing, 1964), 85–86.
2. Mitchell, *Black Preaching*, 29.
3. Bennett, *The Negro Mood*.
4. Labov and Waletzky, "Narrative Analysis," 21–22.

Bibliography

Aarne, Antti. *Verzeichnis der Märchentypen* (Helsinki: Folklore Fellows Communications, 1910).

Abrahams, Roger D. "Playing the Dozens." *Journal of American Folklore* 75 (July/September 1962): 209–20.

———. "Public Drama and Common Values in Two Caribbean Islands." *Transaction* 5 (July/August 1968): 62–71.

———. "Can You Dig It? Aspects of the African Esthetic in Afro-America." Paper presented at the African Folklore Institute, Indiana University, Bloomington, July 16–18, 1970.

———. *Deep Down in the Jungle: Negro Narrative Folklore from the Streets of Philadelphia.* 1st rev. ed. Chicago: Aldine, 1970.

———. "Patterns of Performance in the West Indies." In *Afro-American Anthropology: Contemporary Perspectives*, edited by Norman Whitten, Jr., and John F. Szwed. New York: Free Press, 1970.

———. "A Performance-Centered Approach to Gossip." *Man* 5 (June 1970): 290–301.

Abrahams, Roger D., and John Szwed, eds. *Afro-American Folk Culture: An Annotated Bibliography.* 2 vols. Philadelphia: Institute for the Study of Human Issues, 1978.

Adams, Edward C. L. *Congaree Sketches: Scenes from Negro Life in the Swamps of the Congaree and Tales by Tad and Scip of Heaven and Hell with other Miscellany.* Chapel Hill: University of North Carolina Press, 1927.

———. *Nigger to Nigger.* New York: Scribner's, 1928.

Albert, Ethel M. "Conceptual Systems in Africa." In *The African Experience*, edited by John N. Paden and Edward W. Soja. Evanston: Northwestern University Press, 1970.

Allen, Helen Bernice. "The Minister of the Gospel in North American Fiction." Master's thesis, Fisk University, 1937.

Anderson, Robert. *From Slavery to Affluence: Memoirs of Robert Anderson, Ex-Slave.* Hemingford, Nebr.: Hemingford Ledger, 1927.

Armstrong, Orlando Kay. *Old Massa's People: The Old Slaves Tell Their Story.* Indianapolis: Bobbs-Merrill, 1931.

Armstrong, Robert Plant. *The Affecting Presence: An Essay in Humanistic Anthropology.* Urbana: University of Illinois Press, 1971.

———. *Wellspring: On the Myth and Source of Culture.* Berkeley and Los Angeles: University of California Press, 1975.

Bacon, Alice Mabel. "Work and Methods of the Hampton Folklore Society." *Journal of American Folklore* 11 (January/March 1898): 19–21.

Baer, Hans A., *The Black Spiritual Movement: A Religious Response to Racism* (Knoxville: The University of Tennessee Press, 1984).

Baker, Houston A. *Long Black Song: Essays in Black American Literature and Culture.* Charlottesville: University Press of Virginia, 1972.

———. *The Journey Back: Issues in Black Literature and Criticism.* Chicago: University of Chicago Press, 1980.

Banks, William L. *The Black Church in the United States: Its Origin, Growth, Contribution and Outlook.* Chicago: Moody Press, 1972.

Bare, Paul W. "The Negro Church in Philadelphia." Master's thesis, Drew University, 1931.

Barrett, Leonard E. *Soul-Force: African Heritage in Afro-American Religion.* Garden City: Anchor Books, 1974.

Barth, Fredrik, ed. *Ethnic Groups and Boundaries: The Social Organization of Cultural Difference.* Boston: Little, Brown, 1974.

Bascom, William R. "The Relationship of Yoruba Folklore to Divining." *Journal of American Folklore* 56 (April/June 1943): 127–31.

———. "Yoruba Acculturation in Cuba." In *Les Afro-Americans.* Memoires de l'Institut Fondamental d'Afrique Noire, no. 27. Dakar, 1953.

———. "Verbal Art." *Journal of American Folklore* 68 (April/June 1955): 245–52.

———. *Ifa Divination: Communication between Gods and Men in West Africa.* Bloomington: Indiana University Press, 1969.

Bastide, Roger. *Les Ameriques noires: Les civilisations africains dans le nouveau monde.* Paris: Payot, 1958.

Bauman, Richard. "Verbal Art as Performance." *American Anthropologist* 77 (June 1975): 290–311.

———, ed. "Differential Identity and the Social Base of Folklore." *Journal of American Folklore* 84 (January/March 1971): 31–41.

Beals, Ralph L. "Who Will Rule Research?" *Psychology Today* (September 1970): 44–47, 75ff.

Beckett, Lemuel M. *True Worshippers, A Sermon.* Philadelphia: A.M.E. Book Concern, 1911.

Bell, Bernard W. *The Folk Roots of Contemporary Afro-American Poetry.* Detroit: Broadside Press, 1974.

Ben-Amos, Dan. "Analytic Categories and Ethnic Genres." *Genre* 2 (September 1969): 275–301.

———. "Towards a Definition of Folklore in Context." *Journal of American Folklore* 84 (January/March 1971): 3–15.

Ben-Amos, Dan, and Kenneth S. Goldstein, eds. *Folklore: Communication and Performance.* The Hague: Mouton, 1975.

Bennet, Winifred De Witt. "A Survey of American Negro Oratory." Master's thesis, George Washington University, 1935.

Bennett, Lerone, Jr. *The Negro Mood, and Other Essays.* Chicago: Johnson Publishing, 1964.

Bernstein, B. "Some Sociological Determinants of Perception: An Inquiry into

Sub-Cultural Differences." In *Readings in the Sociology of Language*, edited by Joshua Fishman. The Hague: Mouton, 1968.

Beynon, Erdmann Doane. "The Voodoo Cult among Negro Migrants in Detroit." *American Journal of Sociology* 4 (May 1938): 894–907.

Blackburn, George A. *The Life and Work of John L. Girardeau, D.D., L.L.D.* Columbia, S.C.: State, 1916.

Blackwell, George L. *The Model Homestead: Three Pointed, Practical and Picturesque Sermons on the Parable of the Prodigal Son*. Boston: H. Marshall, 1893.

Blassingame, John W. *The Slave Community: Plantation Life in the Antebellum South*. New York: Oxford University Press, 1972.

Boedker, Laurits. *European Folktales*. Copenhagen: Folklore Associates, 1963.

Bohannan, Laura. "Shakespeare in the Bush." *Natural History* 75 (August/September 1966): 28–33.

Bontemps, Arna. "Rock Church, Rock," in *Anthology of American Negro Literature*, edited by Sylvester C. Watkins. New York: Modern Library, 1944.

Borders, Williams Holmes. *What Is That in Thine Hand? And Other Sermons*. N.P., n.d.

Borgatti, Jean M. "The Festival as Art Event, Form and Iconography: Olimi Festival in Okpella Clan, Etsako Division, Midwest State Nigeria." Ph.D. diss., University of California at Los Angeles, 1976.

———. "Okpella Masking Traditions." *African Arts* 9 (July 1976): 24–33.

———. "Dead Mothers of Okpella." *African Arts* 12 (August 1979): 48–57.

———. "Okpella Masks: In Search of the Parameters of the Beautiful and the Grotesque." *Studies in Visual Communication* 8 (Summer 1982): 28–40.

Bowling, Richard H. *"Closed Doors That Do Not Deter The Master," A Radio Sermon . . . And Activities of the First Baptist Church*. Norfolk: Guide Publishing, n.d.

Bracey, John H. "Theories of African-American History." Paper presented at a conference entitled "The African Mind in the New World," Rutgers University, November 18–20, 1976.

Bradford, Amory. *Oakland's Not for Burning*. New York: McKay, 1968.

Brawley, Edward M., ed. *The Negro Baptist Pulpit*. Philadelphia: American Baptist Publication Society, 1890.

Brewer, J. Mason. *The Word on the Brazos: Negro Preacher Tales from the Brazos Bottoms of Texas*. Austin: University of Texas Press, 1953.

———. *American Negro Folklore*. Chicago: Quadrangle Books, 1968.

Brooks, Charles H. *Official History of the First African Baptist Church, Philadelphia, Pennsylvania*. Philadelphia: n.p., 1922.

Brooks, Gwendolyn. *In the Mecca*. New York: Harper and Row, 1968.

Brooks, Phillip. *Lectures on Preaching*. New York: Dutton, 1894.

Brooks, Walter H. "The Evolution of the Negro Baptist Church." *Journal of Negro History* 3 (January 1922): 11–22.

Brown, L. B. "The Structure of Religious Belief." *Journal for the Scientific Study of Religion* 5 (Spring 1966): 259–72.

Brown, Sterling A. "Negro Folk Expression." *Phylon* 14 (Spring 1953): 50–60.

Buhle, Paul. "Marxism and Popular Culture." *Review of Radical History* (Spring 1974): pp. 4–5.

Burr, Nelson R. "The Negro Church." *Critical Bibliography of Religion in America*. Vol. 4. Princeton: Princeton University Press, 1961.

Bynum, David E. "The Generic Nature of Oral Epic Poetry." *Genre* 2 (September 1969): 236–58.

———. "Thematic Sequences and Transformation of Character in Oral Narrative Tradition." *Filoloski Pregled* (Belgrade) 8 (1970): i–ii, 1–21.

———. "Oral Evidence and the Historian: Problems and Methods." *Journal of the Folklore Institute* 8 (August/December 1971): 82–84.

———. Review of *Heroic Poetry of the Basotho*, by Daniel P. Kunene. *Research in African Literature* 4 (Spring 1973): 114–16.

Caldwell, Lewis A. H. *The Policy King*. Chicago: New Vista Publishing House, 1945.

Calley, Malcolm J. C. *God's People West Indian Pentecostal Sects in London, England*. London: Oxford University Press, 1965.

Campbell, Ernest Q., and Thomas F. Pettigrew. "Racial and Moral Crisis: The Role of Little Rock Ministers." *American Journal of Sociology* 64 (March 1959): 509–16.

Cantril, Hadley. *The Psychology of Social Movements*. New York: Wiley, 1941.

Carawan, Guy, and Candie Carawan. *Ain't You Got a Right to the Tree of Life?—The People of Johns Island: Their Faces, Their Words and Their Songs*. New York: Simon and Shuster, 1966.

Castleman, Rev. T. T. "Plain Sermons for Servants: A Review." *Church Review* 4 (1852): 368–83.

Chamberlain, Alexander F. "Record of Negro Folk-lore." *Journal of American Folklore* 16 (October/December 1903): 273.

Chapman, Abraham. *Black Voices*. New York: New American Library, 1968.

Chappelle, E. *The Voice of God*. New York: Carlton Press, 1963.

Chatman, Seymour B. *Literary Style: A Symposium*. New York: Oxford University Press, 1971.

Clark, Elmer T. *The Small Sects in America*. Nashville: Abingdon Press, 1937.

Colby, B. N. "Ethnographic Semantics: A Preliminary Survey." *Current Anthropology* 7 (February 1966): 3–32.

Collier, Betty J. "Capitalism and the African-American Slave." Paper presented at a conference entitled "The African Mind in the New World," Rutgers University, November 18–20, 1976.

Cone, James H. *The Spirituals and the Blues*. New York: Seabury Press, 1972.

Connelly, Bridget. "Oral Poetics: The Arab Case." Paper presented at the annual meeting of the Modern Language Association, New York, December 1974.

Courlander, Harold. *The Drum and the Hoe: Life and Lore of the Haitian People*. Berkeley/Los Angeles: University of California Press, 1960.

Cothran, Kay L. "Talking Trash in the Okefenokee Swamp Rim, Georgia." *Journal of American Folklore* 87 (October/December 1974): 340–56.

Crane, Thomas F. "Medieval Sermon Books and Stories." *Proceedings* 21 (1883 and 1884): 49–78.
———. *The Exempla, or Illustrative Stories from the Sermones Vulgare of Jacques de Vitry.* London, 1890.
———. "Medieval Sermon Books and Stories since 1883." *Proceedings* 56 (1917).
Crowley, Daniel J. *I Could Talk Old-Story Good: Creativity in Bahamian Folklore.* Berkeley and Los Angeles: University of California Press, 1966.
Cullen, Countee. *One Way to Heaven.* New York: Harper, 1932.
Culley, Robert C. *Studies in the Structure of Hebrew Narratives.* Philadelphia: Fortress Press, 1979.
Curschmann, Michael. "The Concept of Formula as an Impediment to Our Understanding of Medieval Oral Paper." Paper presented at the annual meeting of the Modern Language Association, New York, December 1974.
Dance, Daryl Cumber. *Shuckin' and Jivin': Folklore from Contemporary Black Americans.* Bloomington: Indiana University Press, 1978.
Daniel, Vattel E. "Ritual and Stratification in Chicago Negro Churches." *American Sociological Review* 7 (June 1942): 353–61.
Davis, Gerald L. "An Analysis of Afro-American Sermons." Master's thesis, University of California at Berkeley, 1975.
Davis, Lawrence A. "The Negro Interpretation of the Bible." Master's thesis, University of Kansas, 1941.
Day, Gregory. "Afro-Carolinian Art: Towards the History of a Southern Expressive Tradition." *Contemporary Arts/Southeast,* January/February 1978, pp. 10–21.
Diop, Cheikh Anta. *L'unite culturelle de l'Afrique noire.* Paris: Presence Africaine, 1959.
———. *The African Origin of Civilization: Myth or Reality?* Translated and edited by Mercer Cook. New York: Lawrence Hill, 1974.
Dollard, John. "The Dozens: The Dialect of Insult." *American Imago* 1 (November 1939): 3–24.
Dorson, Richard M. *American Negro Folktales.* Greenwich, Conn.: Fawcett, 1967.
Douglass, William. *Sermons Preached.* Philadelphia: n.p., 1854.
Drake, St. Clair, and Horace Cayton. *Black Metropolis.* New York: Harcourt, Brace, 1945.
Dressler, Janet N. "Exempla Usage in Catholic Parochial Schools." *Folklore Forum* 8 (November 1975): 130–41.
Du Bois, W. E. B. *The Negro Church.* Atlanta: Atlanta University, 1903.
———. *The Souls of Black Folk.* Chicago, 1903.
———. *Economic Cooperation among Negro Americans.* Atlanta: Atlanta University Press, 1907.
———. *Efforts for Social Betterment among Negro Americans.* Atlanta: Atlanta University Press, 1909.
———. Review of *The Book of American Negro Spirituals* (James Weldon Johnson and J. Rosamond Johnson). *Crisis* 31 (November 1925): 31.

————. *Black Reconstruction*. New York: Harcourt, 1935.

DuFrerme, Michael. *Pour l'homme*. Paris: du Sevil, 1968.

Dunbar, Paul Laurence. *The Completed Poems of Paul Laurence Dunbar*. New York: Dodd, Mead, 1913.

————. *In Old Plantation Days*. New York: Dodd, Mead, 1913.

Dundes, Alan. "From Etic to Emic Units in the Structural Study of Folktales." *Journal of American Folklore* 75 (April/June 1962): 95–105.

————. "Texture, Text and Context." *Southern Folklore Quarterly* 28 (December 1964): 251–65.

————. "Metafolklore and Oral Literary Criticism." *Monist* 50 (October 1966): 505–16.

————. "Introduction to the Second Edition." *Morphology of the Folktale*, by Vladimir Propp. Austin: University of Texas Press, 1968.

————. "The Number Three in American Culture," in *Every Man His Way*. Englewood Cliffs: Prentice-Hall, 1968.

————. "The Devolutionary Premise in Folklore Theory." *Journal of the Folklore Institute* 6 (June 1969): 5–19.

————. Headnote to "Jokes and Black Consciousness: A Collection with Interviews," by Paulette Cross. In *Mother Wit from The Laughing Barrel: Readings in the Interpretation of Afro-American Folklore*, edited by Alan Dundes. Englewood Cliffs: Prentice-Hall, 1973.

Ebin, David, ed. *The Drug Experience*. New York: Grove Press, 1965.

Echeruo, M. J. C. "American Negro Poetry." *Phylon* 24 (Spring 1968): 62–68.

Eddington, Neil A. "The Urban Plantation: An Ethnography of an Oral Tradition in a Negro Community." Ph.D. diss., University of California at Berkeley, 1967.

Edmonson, M. S. "Play: Games, Gossip and Humor." *Handbook of Middle American Indians*, ed. Manning Nash. Austin: University of Texas Press, 1966.

Eighmy, John Lee. *Churches in Cultural Captivity: A History of the Social Attitudes of Southern Baptists*. Knoxville: University of Tennessee Press, 1972.

Eliade, Mircea. *The Sacred and the Profane*. Translated by Willard R. Trask. New York: Harper and Row, 1959.

Ellis, Alfred B. *The Tshi-Speaking Peoples of the Gold Coast of West Africa*. London, 1887.

Ellison, Ralph. *Invisible Man*. New York: New American Library, 1952.

Erb, John David. "Is There a Positive Correlation between Successful Preaching and the Use of Vivid Imagery Word Concepts?" Master's thesis, Ohio State University, 1938.

Erikson, Eric H. *Identity and the Life Cycle*. New York: Norton, 1959.

Faduma, Orishatukeh. "Some Defects of the Negro Church." *The Southern Workman* 32 (April 1903); 229–32.

Faulk, John Henry. "Ten Negro Sermons." Master's thesis, University of Texas, 1940.

Faulkner, William. *The Sound and the Fury*. New York: Random House, 1929.

Fauset, Arthur Huff. *Black Gods of the Metropolis.* Philadelphia: University of Pennsylvania Press, 1944.

Fearon, Henry Bradshaw. *Sketches of America.* London: Longman, Hurst, Reese, Orne and Brown, 1819.

Feldman, Susan. *African Myths and Tales.* New York: Dell, 1963.

Felton, Ralph A. *They Are My Brothers: A Study of 570 Negro Churches and 1542 Negro Houses in the Rural South.* Madison: Drew Theological Seminary, n.d.

Ferguson, Marilyn. *The Aquarian Conspiracy: Personal and Social Transformation in the 1980s.* Los Angeles: J. P. Tarcher, 1980.

Ferm, Virgilius, ed. *Encyclopedia of Religion.* New York: Philosophical Library, 1945.

Fernandez, James W. "Unbelievably Subtle Words: Representation and Integration in the Sermons of an African Reformative Cult." *History of Religions* 6 (August 1966): 43–69.

————. "Equatorial Excursions: The Folklore of Narcotic-Inspired Visions in an African Religious Movement." In *African Folklore*, edited by Richard Dorson. Bloomington: Indiana University Press, 1972.

Fichter, Joseph. "Negro Spirituals and Catholicism." *Interracial Review* 35 (September 1962): 200–203.

Finnegan, Ruth. *Oral Literature in Africa.* New York: Oxford University Press, 1970.

Fisher, Francis D. *An Impression of "The Oakland Project": Considerations Important to the Design of Projects Linking Universities and City Government.* Washington, D.C.: Urban Institute, 1972.

Fisher, Miles Mark. *The Master's Slave Elijah John Fisher.* Philadelphia: Judson Press, 1922.

————. *Negro Slave Songs in the United States.* Ithaca: Cornell University Press, 1953.

Fishwick, Marshall, ed. *Remus, Rastus, Revolution.* Bowling Green, Ohio: Bowling Green University Popular Press, 1971.

Foley, John Miles. "The Traditional Structure of Utterance in Ibro Basic's 'Alagic Aliza and Velagic Selim.'" Paper presented at the annual meeting of the Modern Language Association, New York, December 1976.

Forsythe, Dennis. "The 'Black Perspective' as a Sociological Paradigm: A Marxist Critique." Paper presented at a conference entitled "The African Mind in the New World," Rutgers University, November 18–20, 1976.

Fortes, Meyer. *Oedipus and Job in West African Religion.* Cambridge: Cambridge University Press, 1959.

Frank, Waldo. *In the American Jungle.* New York: Farrar and Rinehart, 1937.

Franklin, John Hope. "The Past in the Future of the South." In *Continuity and Change in the South*, edited by Edgar Thompson. Durham: Duke University Press, 1965.

Frazier, E. Franklin. *The Negro Family in the United States.* Chicago: University of Chicago Press, 1939.

————. *The Negro in the United States.* New York: Macmillan, 1957.

————. *The Negro Church in America*. New York: Schocken, 1964.

Freeman, Donald C., ed. *Linguistic and Literary Styles*. New York: Holt, Rinehart and Winston, 1970.

Friedman, Albert B. "The Formulaic Improvisation Theory of Ballad Tradition—A Counterstatement." *Journal of American Folklore* 74 (April/June 1961): 113–15.

Fry, Donald K. "Aesthetic Applications of Oral-Formulaic Theory: Judith 199–216a." Ph.D. diss., University of California at Berkeley, 1966.

————. "The Present State of Oral Literary Studies in Old English." Paper presented at the annual meeting of the Modern Language Association, New York, December 1974.

Fry, John R. *Fire and Blackstone*. Philadelphia: Lippincott, 1969.

Fugate, Joe K. *The Psychological Basis of Herder's Aesthetics*. The Hague: Mouton, 1966.

Gayle, Addison, Jr. *Black Expression: Essays by and about Black Americans in the Creative Arts*. New York: Weybright and Talley, 1969.

————. *The Black Aesthetic*. Garden City: Doubleday, 1971.

————. "Reclaiming the Southern Experience: The Black Aesthetic Ten Years later." *Black World* 23 (September 1974): 20–29.

Gillen, John, and E. J. Murphy. "Notes on Southern Culture Patterns." *Social Forces* 29 (May 1951): 422–32.

Glennie, Alexander. *Sermons Preached on Plantations*. 1844.

Gluckman, Max. "Gossip and Scandal." *Current Anthropology* 3 (June 1963): 307–16.

Goffman, Erving. *Interaction Ritual, Essays on Face-to-Face Behavior*. Chicago: Aldine, 1967.

Goldstein, Kenneth S. *A Guide for Fieldworkers in Folklore*. New York: Folklore Associates, 1964.

Gonzales, Ambrose E. *With Aesop Along the Black Border*. New York: Negro University Press, 1924; reprinted 1969.

Goodenough, Ward. "Frontiers of Cultural Anthropology: Social Organization." *Proceedings of the American Philosophical Society* 113 (October 1969): 329–35.

Grambo, Ronald. "Note on Alan Dundes' Devolutionary Premise." *Folklore Forum* 3 (1970): 57–58.

Gray, Bennison. "Repetition in Oral Literature." *Journal of American Folklore* 84 (January/March 1971): 289–303.

Grimes, Terry K. "Sermon Artistry of the Black Preacher." Term paper, Indiana University, December 1980.

Gumperz, John J. "Types of Linguistic Communities." In *Readings in the Sociology of Language*, ed. Joshua Fishman. The Hague: Mouton, 1968.

Gustafson, James M. "The Clergy in the United States." *Daedalus* 92 (Fall 1963): 724–44.

Hall, Edward T. *The Hidden Dimension*. Garden City: Doubleday, 1966.

Hamilton, Charles V. *The Black Preacher in America*. New York: Morrow, 1972.

Hannerz, Ulf. "Gossip Networks and Culture in a Black American Ghetto." *Ethnos* 32 (1967): 35–60.

Haralambos, Michael. "Soul Music and Blues: Their Meaning and Relevance in Northern United States Black Ghettos." In *Afro-American Anthropology: Contemporary Perspectives*, edited by Norman Whitten and John F. Szwed. New York: Free Press, 1970.

Harrison, Paul Carter. *Kuntu Drama: Plays of the African Continuum*. New York: Grove Press, 1974.

Harrison, W. P. *The Gospel among the Slaves*. Nashville: Publishing House of the Methodist Episcopal Church, South, 1893.

Hayes, Edward C. *Power Structure and Urban Policy: Who Rules Oakland?* New York: McGraw-Hill, 1971.

Haynes, Edward R. *A Bibliography of Studies Relating to Parry's and Lord's Oral Theory*. Cambridge: Harvard University Printing Office, 1973.

———. *Repetitions and Oral Formula: A Reappraisal*. Paper presented at the annual meeting of the Modern Language Association, New York, December 1976.

Heilbut, Tony. *The Gospel Sound*. New York: Simon and Shuster, 1971.

Henderson, Stephen E. *Understanding the New Black Poetry: Black Speech and Black Music as Poetic References*. New York: Morrow, 1973.

Herskovits, Melville J. "Social History of the Negro." In *Handbook of Social Psychology*, edited by C. Murchison. Worcester: Clark University Press, 1935.

———. *The Myth of the Negro Past*. New York: Harper, 1941.

———. *Trinidad Village*. New York: Knopf, 1947.

Hicks, Henry Beecher, Jr. *Images of the Black Preacher: The Man Nobody Knows*. Valley Forge: Judson Press, 1977.

Higginson, Thomas W. *Army Life in a Black Regiment*. Boston: Fields, Osgood, 1870.

Hilger, Rotha. "The Religious Expression of the Negro." Master's thesis, Vanderbilt University, 1931.

Hill, Mozelle E., and Bevode C. McCall. "Cracker Culture: A Preliminary Definition." *Phylon* 11 (Third Quarter 1950): 223–31.

Holt, Grace Sims. "'Inversion' in Black Communication." *Florida FL Reporter* (Spring/Fall 1971): 41–43, 55.

Hood, James Walker. *The Negro in the Christian Pulpit; or, The Two Characters and Two Destinies Delineated in Twenty-one Practical Sermons*. Raleigh: Edwards Broughton, 1884.

Houis, Maurice. *Anthropologie linguistique de l'Afrique noire*. Paris: Presses universitaires de France, 1971.

Hudson, Charles. "Folk History and Ethnohistory." *Ethnohistory* 13 (Winter/Spring, 1966): 52–70.

Hughes, Langston. *Selected Poems of Langston Hughes*. New York: Knopf, 1959.

Hurston, Zora Neal. *Mules and Men: Negro Folktales and Voodoo in the South*. Philadelphia: Lippincott, 1935. Reprint. New York: Perennial Library, 1970.

————. *Tell My Horse*. Philadelphia: Lippincott and Crowell, 1938. Reprint. Berkeley: Turtle Island, 1981.

————. *The Sanctified Church*. Berkeley: Turtle Island, 1983.

Hymes, Dell H. "The Ethnography of Speaking." *Readings in the Sociology of Language*, edited by Joshua Fishman. The Hague: Mouton, 1968.

————. "Models of the Interaction of Language and Social Life." Philadelphia, University of Pennsylvania. Typescript.

————. "The Use of Anthropology: Critical, Political, Personal." In *Reinventing Anthropology*, edited by Dell Hymes. New York: Random House, 1969.

————. "Linguistic Method of Ethnography." In *Method and Theory in Linguistics*, edited by P. L. Garvin. The Hague: Mouton, 1970.

————. "Morris Swadesh and the First Yale School." In *Origin and Diversification of Languages*, edited by Joel Sherzer. Chicago: Aldine, 1971.

Hymes, Dell H., and John J. Gumperz, eds. *Directions in Sociolinguistics: The Ethnography of Communication*. New York: Holt, Rinehart and Winston, 1972.

Jabbour, Alan A. "Memorial Transmission in Old English Poetry." *Chaucer Review* 3 (Winter, 1969): 174–90.

Jackson, Bruce. *The Negro and His Folklore in Nineteenth Century Periodicals*. Austin: University of Texas Press, 1967.

Jackson, L. P. "Religious Development of the Negro in Virginia from 1760 to 1860." *Journal of Negro History* 16 (April 1931): 168.

Jahoda, Gustav. *The Psychology of Superstition*. Baltimore: Penguin Press, 1969.

James, William. *The Will to Believe, and Other Essays in Popular Philosophy*. New York: Longmans, Green, 1897.

James, Willis Laurence. "The Romance of the Negro Folk Cry in America." *Phylon* 16 (Spring 1955): 15–30.

Johnson, Charles S. *Shadow of the Plantation*. Chicago: University of Chicago Press, 1934.

————. *Growing Up in the Black Belt*. Washington, D.C.: American Council on Education, 1941.

Johnson, Clifton, ed. *God Struck Me Dead: Religious Conversion Experiences and Autobiographies of Negro Ex-Slaves*. Nashville: Fisk University Social Science Institute, 1945.

Johnson, James Weldon. *God's Trombones: Seven Negro Sermons in Verse*. New York: Viking, 1964.

Johnson, Walton. *Worship and Freedom: A Black American Church in Zambia*. New York: Africana Publishing Co., 1977.

Johnston, Ruby F. *The Development of Negro Religion*. New York: Philosophical Library, 1954.

Jones, Absalom, and Richard Allen. "A Narrative of the Proceedings of the Black People, During the Late Awful Calamity in Philadelphia, in the Year, 1793." In *Negro Protest Pamphlets*, edited by Dorothy Porter. New York: Arno Press and the New York Times, 1969.

Jones, Alice Marie. "The Negro Folk Sermon: A Study in the Sociology of Folk Culture." Master's thesis, Fisk University, 1942.

Jones, James H. "Commonplace and Memorization in the Oral Tradition of the English and Scottish Popular Ballads." *Journal of American Folklore* 74 (April/June 1961): 97–112.

Jones, LeRoi. *Blues People: The Negro Experience in White America and the Music That Developed from It.* New York: Morrow 1963.

Jones, William A. *The Gospel and the Ghetto.* Elgin, Ill.: Progressive Baptist Publishing House, 1979.

Joyner, Charles W. "The Unusual Task of the Gospel Preacher: Afro-American Folk Preaching on Sandy Island, South Carolina." Typescript.

Katz, Bernard, ed. *The Social Implications of Early Negro Music in the United States.* New York: Arno Press, 1969.

Keil, Charles. "Motion and Feeling through Music." *Journal of Aesthetics and Art Criticism* 24 (Spring 1966): 337–49.

———. *Urban Blues.* Chicago: University of Chicago Press, 1966.

Kellogg, Robert. "What Is an Oral Epic?" Paper presented at annual meeting of the Modern Language Association, New York, December 27–30, 1976.

Kennard, J., Jr. "Who Are Our National Poets?" *Knickerbocker Magazine* 26 (October 1845): 331–41.

Kent, George. *Blackness and the Adventure of Western Culture.* Chicago: Third World Press, 1972.

Kilham, Elizabeth. "Sketches in Color: IV." *Putnam's Monthly* 15 (March 1870): 304–11.

King, Martin Luther, Jr. *Strength to Love.* New York: Harper and Row, 1963.

Kingsley, Mary H. *West African Studies.* New York: Macmillan, 1968.

Kochman, Thomas, ed. *Rappin' and Stylin' Out: Communication in Urban Black America.* Urbana: University of Illinois Press, 1972.

Kramer, Ralph M. *Participation of the Poor: Comparative Community Case Studies in the War on Poverty.* Englewood Cliffs: Prentice-Hall, 1969.

Kuhn, Thomas S. *The Structure of Scientific Revolutions.* 2d. ed. Chicago: University of Chicago Press, 1970.

Kunene, Daniel P. *Heroic Poetry of the Basotho.* New York: Oxford University Press, 1971.

Kuttner, Gerhard. "Wesen und Formen der deutschen Schwankliteratur des 15. Jahrhunderts." *Germanistische Studien* 152 (1934).

Labov, William. *Language in the Inner City.* Philadelphia: University of Pennsylvania Press, 1972.

Labov, William, Paul Cohen, and Clarence Robins, *A Preliminary Study of the Structure of English Used by Negro and Puerto Rican Speakers in New York City.* Project no. 3091. Washington, D.C.: U.S. Office of Education Cooperative Research, 1965.

Labov, William, and Joshua Waletzky. "Narrative Analysis: Oral Versions of Personal Experience." In *Essays on the Verbal and Visual Arts* (Proceedings of the Annual Spring Meeting of the American Ethnological Society, 1966), edited by June Helm. Seattle: University of Washington Press, 1966.

Lenski, Gerhard. *The Religious Factor: A Sociologist's Inquiry.* Garden City: Doubleday, 1961.

Levine, Lawrence W. *Black Culture and Black Consciousness: Afro-American Folk Thought from Slavery to Freedom.* New York: Oxford University Press, 1977.

Lévi-Strauss, Claude. *The Raw and the Cooked.* New York: Harper and Row, Torchbooks, 1969.

Liebow, Elliot. *Talley's Corner: A Study of Streetcorner Negro Men.* Boston: Little, Brown, 1967.

Lincoln, C. Eric. *The Black Experience in Religion.* Garden City: Doubleday, Anchor, 1974.

Lockley, Edith Alyce. "The Spiritualist Sect in Nashville: A Study in Personality Reorganization." Master's thesis, Fisk University, 1936.

Lomax, Alan. *The Rainbow Sign: A Southern Documentary.* New York: Duell, Sloan and Pearce, 1959.

Lord, Albert B. *The Singer of Tales.* New York: Atheneum, 1965.

Lundin, Robert W. *An Objective Psychology of Music.* New York: Ronald Press, 1953.

McKinney, Samuel B., and Floyd Massey, Jr. *Church Administration in the Black Perspective.* Valley Forge: Judson Press, 1976.

McLaughlin, Wayman B. "Symbolism and Mysticism in the Spirituals." *Phylon* 24 (Spring 1963): 69–77.

Marshall, Paule. *Soul, Clap Hands and Sing.* New York: Antheneum, 1961.

May, L. Carlyle. "A Survey of Glossolalia and Related Phenomena in Non-Christian Religions." *American Anthropologist* 58 (February 1956): 75–96.

Mays, Benjamin E., and Joseph W. Nicholson. *The Negro's Church.* New York: Institute of Social and Religious Research, 1933.

Melton, Gordon J., and James V. Geiser, eds. *A Director of Religious Bodies in the United States.* New York: Garland, 1977.

Merleau-Ponty, Maurice. *The Primacy of Perception and Other Essays.* Evanston: Northwestern University Press, 1964.

Messenger, John. "The Role of the Carver in Anang Society." In *The Traditional Arts in African Societies,* edited by W. D'Azevedo. Bloomington: Indiana University Press, 1973.

Meyer, Paul. *Les contes moralises de Nicole Bozon.* Paris, 1889.

Mezzrow, Milton, "Mezz." *Really the Blues.* New York: Random House, 1946.

Miller, Elizabeth W. *The Negro in America: A Bibliography.* Cambridge: Harvard University Press, 1966.

Minton, William W. "The Fallacy of the Structural Formula." *TAPA* 96 (1965): 241–53.

Mitchell, Henry H. *Black Preaching.* Philadelphia: Lippincott, 1970.

Monroe, Harriet. "Negro Sermons." *Poetry* 30 (August 1927): 291–93.

Moreau de Saint Mery, Mederic Louis Elie. *Description topographie, physique, civile, politique et historique de la partie français de l'isle Dominque 1797–1798.* Philadelphia: William Cobbett, 1799.

Morris, Colon M. *Out of Africa: Sermons for Central Africa*. London: Lutter-worth Press, 1960.

Nagler, Michael N. "Towards a Generative View of the Oral Formula." *TAPA* 98 (1967): 269–311.

National Advisory Commission on Civil Disorders (Kerner Commission). *Report of the National Advisory Commission on Civil Disorders*. Washington, D.C.: U.S. Government Printing Office, 1968.

———. *Supplemental Studies for the National Advisory Commission on Civil Disorders*. Washington, D.C.: U.S. Government Printing Office, 1968.

Nelson, John H. "The Negro Character in American Literature." *Humanistic Studies of the University of Kansas* 4 (1932): 37.

Nelson, M., and Raytha Yokeley. *The Black Church in America*. New York: Basic Books, 1971.

Newell, William Nells. "Myths of Voodoo Worship and Child Sacrifice in Haiti." *Journal of American Folklore* 1 (April/June 1888): 16–30.

———. "Plantation Courtship." *Journal of American Folklore* 7 (April/June 1894): 147–49.

———. "Plantation Courtship II." *Journal of American Folklore* 8 (April/June 1894): 106.

———. "Courtship Formulas of Southern Negroes." *Southern Workman* 1 (1895): 155.

New York Times Book Review. "Poetry and Eloquence of the Negro Preacher." June 19, 1927.

Nicholls, William L. *Housing and Population Tabulations from the 701 Household Survey of Oakland*. Berkeley: University of California Survey Research Center, 1967.

Oakland (California) City Planning Department, 701 Division. *Oakland's Housing Supply: Cost, Condition, Composition, 1960–1985*. Oakland: Oakland City Planning Department, 1968.

———. *West Oakland: A 701 Subarea Report*. Oakland: Oakland City Planning Department, 1969.

Oliver, Paul. *Conversation with the Blues*. New York: Horizon Press, 1965.

———. *Screening the Blues*. London: Cassell, 1968.

Olmsted, David L. "Comparative Notes on Yoruba and Lucumi." *Language* 29, vol. 2 (1953): 157–64.

Ong, Walter S. "World as View and World as Event." *American Anthropologist* 71 (August 1969): 634–47.

O'Reilly, Aida Takla. "The Survival of African Folktales in the New World." *PASS: A Journal of the Black Experience and Pan-African Issues* 1 (Winter 1975): 103–13.

Oster, Harry. "The Blues as a Genre." *Genre* 2 (September 1969): 259–74.

———. *Living Country Blues*. Baton Rouge: Louisiana State University Press, 1970.

Palmer, Robert. "Trance Music—A Trend of the 1970's." *New York Times*, January 12, 1975.

Payne, Daniel A. *History of the African Methodist Episcopal Church.* Nashville: A.M.E. Sunday School Union, 1891.

Parry, Milman. "Studies in the Epic Technique of Oral Verse-Making I: Homer and Homeric Style." *Harvard Studies in Classical Philology* 41 (1930).

p'Bitek, Okot. *African Religions in Western Scholarship.* Kampala, Nairobi, Dar-es-Salaam: East Africa Literature Bureau, 1970.

Phillips, Charles Henry. *From the Farm to the Bishopric: An Autobiography.* Nashville: Parthenon Press, 1932.

Philpot, William M., ed. *Best Black Sermons.* Valley Forge: Judson Press, 1972.

Pike, Kenneth L. *Language in Relation to a Unified Theory of the Structure of Human Behavior.* Glendale: Summer Institute in Linguistics, 1954. Reissued with revisions. 2nd rev. edition. The Hague: Mouton, 1967.

Pipes, William H. *Say Amen, Brother! Old-Time Negro Preaching: A Study in American Frustration.* New York: William-Frederick Press, 1951.

Porter, James A. "Four Problems in the History of Negro Art." *Journal of Negro History* 27 (January 1942): 9–37.

Powdermaker, Hortense. *After Freedom: A Cultural Study of the Deep South.* New York: Viking, 1939.

Powell, Adam Clayton. *Keep the Faith, Baby!* New York: Trident, 1967.

Pressman, Jeffrey L., and Aaron Wildavsky. *Implementation: How Great Expectations in Washington Are Dashed in Oakland; or, Why It's Amazing That Federal Programs Work at All, This Being the Saga of the Economic Development Administration as Told by Two Sympathetic Observers Who Seek to Build Morals on a Foundation of Ruined Hopes.* Berkeley: University of California Press, 1973.

Propp, Vladmir. *Morphology of the Folktale.* 2d ed. Austin: University of Texas Press, 1968.

Puckett, Newbell Miles. *Folk Beliefs of the Southern Negroes.* Chapel Hill: University of North Carolina Press, 1926.

———. "Religious Folk-Beliefs of Whites and Negroes." *Journal of Negro History* 16 (January 1939): 9–35.

Rasky, Frank. "Harlem's Religious Zealots." *Tomorrow* 9 (November 1949): 11–17.

Rather, Lois. *Oakland's Image: A History of Oakland, California.* Oakland: Rather Press, 1972.

Reid, Ida DeAugustine. "Let Us Prey!" *Opportunity* 4 (September 1926): 274–78.

Richardson, Harry V. *Dark Glory: A Picture of the Church among Negroes in the Rural South.* New York: Friendship Press, 1947.

Rosenberg, Bruce A. *The Art of the American Folk Preacher.* New York: Oxford University Press, 1970.

———. "The Formulaic Quality of Spontaneous Sermons." *Journal of American Folklore* 83 (January/March 1970): 3–20.

———. "The Genre of the Folk Sermon." *Genre* 4 (June 1971): 189–211.

Rowland, Ida. "Study of Rituals and Ceremonies of Negroes in Omaha." Master's thesis, Omaha University, 1938.

Ruby, Jay, ed. *A Crack in the Mirror: Reflexive Perspectives in Anthropology.* Philadelphia: University of Pennsylvania Press, 1982.

Samarin, William J. "Orderly Theory with Disorderly Data." Paper presented at the annual meeting of the American Anthropological Association, New York, 1971.

———. *Tongues of Men and Angels: The Religious Language of Pentecostalism.* New York: Macmillan, 1972.

Sapir, Edward. *Language.* New York: Harcourt, Brace and Co., 1939.

———. "Culture, Genuine and Spurious." *American Journal of Sociology* 29 (January 1924): 401–29.

———. "Sound Patterns in Language." *Language* 1 (1925): 37–51.

———. "Speech as a Personality Trait." *American Journal of Sociology* 32 (May 1927): 892–905.

———. "The Status of Linguistics as a Science." *Language* 5 (1929): 207–14.

———. "Cultural Anthropology and Psychiatry." *Journal of Abnormal and Social Psychology* 27 (1932): 229–42.

Scott, Manuel Lee. *From a Black Brother.* Nashville: Broadman Press, 1971.

———. *The Gospel from the Ghetto: Sermons from a Black Pulpit.* Nashville: Broadman Press, 1973.

"Sermon of an Ante-Bellum Negro Preacher." *Southern Workman* 30, pp. 655–58.

"Sermons and Prayers." *Southern Workman* 24, pp. 59–61.

Shabazz, Betty. *Malcolm X on Afro-American History.* New York: Merit Publishers, 1967.

Sherwood, W. H. *Sherwood's Solid Shot: A Few of the Sermons of the Negro Evangelist as Preached by Him in Revival Meetings, North, South, East and West, and Reported by George F. Thompson . . . Styled Dead Shots.* Boston: McDonald, Gill, 1891.

Simmons, Donald C. "Possible West African Sources for the American Negro 'Dozens.'" *Journal of American Folklore* 76 (October/December 1963): 339–40.

Smith, Barbara H. *Poetic Closures: A Study of How Poems End.* Chicago: University of Chicago Press, 1968.

Smith, John A., and Bruce A. Rosenberg. "Thematic Structure in Four Fundamentalist Sermons." *Western Folklore* 34 (July 1975): 201–14.

Smith, Robert Jerome. "The Structure of Esthetic Response." *Journal of American Folklore* 84 (January/March 1971): 68–79.

Southern, Eileen. *The Music of Black Americans: A History.* New York: Norton, 1971.

Spillers, Hortense J. "Martin Luther King and the Style of the Black Sermon." *Black Scholar* 3 (September 1971): 14–27.

Steiner, R. "Sol Lockhart's Call." *Journal of American Folklore* 13 (January/March 1900): 67–70.

Stoney, Samuel Gaillard, and Gertrude Mathews Shelby. *Black Genesis: A Chronicle*. New York: Macmillan, 1930.

Strauss, David. "Music: A Physical Approach." *Pennsylvania Triangle* 57 (October 1969): 17–21.

Sutherland, Robert L. *An Analysis of Negro Churches in Chicago*. Ph.D. diss., University of Chicago, 1930.

Sutton-Smith, Brian. "Expressive Profile." *Journal of American Folklore* 84 (January/March 1971): 80–92.

Szwed, John F. "Gossip, Drinking and Social Control: Consensus and Communication in a Newfoundland Parish." *Ethnology* 5 (October 1966): 434–41.

———. "Musical Adaptation among Afro-Americans." *Journal of American Folklore* 82 (April/June 1969): 112–21.

———. "An American Anthropological Dilemma: The Politics of Afro-American Culture." In *Reinventing Anthropology*, edited by Dell Hymes. New York: Pantheon, 1974.

Szwed, John F., and Roger D. Abrahams, eds. *Discovering Afro-Americans*. Leiden: E. G. Brill, 1975.

Talley, Thomas W. *Negro Folk Rhymes Wise and Otherwise, with a Study*. New York: Macmillan, 1922. Reprint. Port Washington, N.Y.: Kennikat Press, 1968.

———. "The Origin of Negro Traditions, Part I." *Phylon* (4th quarter, 1942): 371–76.

———. "The Origin of Negro Traditions, Part II." *Phylon* (1st quarter, 1943): 30–38.

Taylor, Clyde. "'Salt Peanuts,' Sound and Sense in African/American Oral/Musical Creativity." *Callaloo* 5, no. 16 (October 1982): 1–11.

Thomas, Edgar G. *The First African Baptist Church of North America*. Savannah, 1925.

Thompson, Robert Farris. "An Aesthetic of the Cool: West African Dance." *African Forum* 2 (1966).

Thompson, Stith. *Types of the Folk-Tale*. Helsinki: Folklore Fellows Communications, 1928.

———, ed. *Four Symposia in Folklore*. Bloomington: Indiana University Press, 1953.

Thurman, Howard. *Deep River: Reflections of the Religious Insight of Certain of the Negro Spirituals*. New York: Harper, 1955.

———. *The Growing Edge*. New York: Harper, 1956.

Tindley, C. A. *Book of Sermons*. Philadelphia: Tindley, 1932.

Tubach, Frederich C. "History of the Exemplum in Germany to 1500." Ph.D. diss., University of California at Berkeley, 1957.

———. "Exempla in the Decline." *Traditio* 18 (1962): 407–11.

———. *Index Exemplorium: A Handbook of Medieval Religious Tales*. Helsinki: Folklore Fellows Communications, 1969.

Turner, James, and W. Eric Perkins. "Towards a Critique of Social Science." *Black Scholar* 7 (April 1976): 2–11.

U.S. Commission on Civil Rights, *Hearing before the United States Commission on Civil Rights* (San Francisco, California, May 1–3, 1967, and Oakland, California, May 4–6, 1977). Washington, D.C.: U.S. Government Printing Office, 1967.

U.S. Office of Economic Opportunity. *Maps of Poverty*. Washington, D.C.: U.S. Bureau of the Census, 1966.

Uya, Okon Edit. "The Mind of the Slaves as Revealed in Their Songs: An Interpretive Essay." *Current Bibliography of African Affairs* 5 (1972): 6–7.

Vajda, Laszlo. "A neprazji anyaggyujtes modszere es jelentosege" (The method and importance of ethnographic data-collecting). *Ethnographia* 65 (1954): 1–19.

Vass, Winifred Kellersberger, *The Bantu-Speaking Heritage of the United States*. Los Angeles: University of California, Center for Afro-American Studies, 1979.

Wade, Melvin, and Margaret Wade. "So We Can Make Yourself and Give Yourself a Mighty Name, Pronominal Innovation by a Black Preacher." University of Texas, Austin, 1976. Typescript.

Walker, Sheila S. *Ceremonial Spirit Possession in African and Afro-America*. Leiden: E. J. Brill, 1972.

Walker, Wyatt Tee. *Somebody's Calling My Name*. Valley Forge: Judson Press, 1979.

———. "Song, Sermon and the Spoken Word: A Symposium on the Folk Base of Black American Literature." *SAGALA, A Journal of Arts and Ideas* (Summer 1980): 12–20.

Washington, Joseph R. *Black Religion: The Negro and Christianity in the United States*. Boston: Beacon Press, 1964.

———. *The Politics of God: The Future of the Black Church*. Boston: Beacon Press, 1967.

Waterman, Richard A. "African Influence on the Music of the Americas." In *Mother Wit from the Laughing Barrel: Readings in the Interpretation of Afro-American Folklore*, edited by Alan Dundes. Englewood Cliffs: Prentice-Hall, 1972.

Watson, James V. *Tales and Takings, Sketches and Incidents from the Itinerant and Educational Budget*. New York: Carlton and Porter, 1856.

Weatherford, Willis Duke. *American Churches and the Negroes: An Historical Study from Early Slave Days to the Present*. Boston: Christopher, 1957.

Webber, Ruth. "Theoretical Studies in Hispanic Oral Literature: Accomplishments and Perspectives." Paper presented at the annual meeting of the Modern Language Association, New York, December 1974.

Weber-Kellerman, Ingeborg. "Probleme interethnischen Forschungen in Sudost-Europa." *Ethnologia Europea* 1 (1967): 218–31.

Welter, Jean Thiebaut. *L'exemplum dans la litterature religieuse et didactique du moyen age*. Paris: Bibliotheque d'histoire Ecclesiastique de France, 1927.

Whaley, Marcellus S. *The Old Types Pass Away: Gullah Sketches of the Carolina Sea Islands*. Boston: Christopher, 1922.

White, Marilyn M. "Ethnolinguistics: A Brief Analysis of 'You' Sermons and Black Baptist Religion." University of Texas, Austin. Typescript.

White, Newman I. *American Negro Folk-Songs*. Hatboro: Folklore Associates, 1965.

Wicks, Harry M. "From War Plays to Jazz." *Communist*, August 16, 1919.

Wiggins, William H. Review of *The Art of the American Folk Preacher*, by Bruce A. Rosenberg. *Folklore Forum* 4 (May/July 1971): 88–89.

———. "The Structure and Dynamics of Folklore in the Novel Form: The Case of John O. Killens." *Keystone Folklore Quarterly* 17 (Fall 1972): 92–118.

Wilgus, D. K. "The Negro-White Spiritual." In *Mother Wit from the Laughing Barrel: Readings in the Interpretation of Afro-American Folklore*, edited by Alan Dundes. Englewood Cliffs: Prentice-Hall, 1972.

Williams, Chancellor. *Have You Been to the River?* New York: Exposition Press, 1952.

Williams, Ethel L. *Biographical Dictionary of Negro Ministers*. New York: Scarecrow Press, 1965.

Williams, Melvin D. *On The Street Where I Lived*. Case Studies in Cultural Anthropology. New York: Holt, Rinehart and Winston, 1981.

Wilson, Gold Refined. "The Religion of the American Negro Slave: His Attitude toward Life and Death." *Journal of Negro History* 8 (January 1923): 41–71.

Winckel, Fritz. *Music, Sound and Sensation—A Modern Exposition*. Translated by Thomas Binkley. New York: Dover, 1967.

Wolfram, Walter A. *A Sociolinguistic Description of Detroit Negro Speech*. Washington, D.C.: Center for Applied Linguistics, 1969.

Woodson, Carter G. *A Century of Negro Migration*. Washington, D.C.: Association for the Study of Negro Life and History, 1918.

———. *The Education of the Negro Prior to 1861*. Washington, D.C.: Associated Publishers, 1919.

———. *The History of the Negro Church*. Washington, D.C.: Associated Publishers, 1921.

———. *Negro Orators and Their Orations*. Washington, D.C.: Associated Publishers, 1925.

———, ed. *The Mind of the Negro Reflected in Letters Written during the Crisis, 1800–1860*. Washington, D.C.: Association for the Study of Negro Life and History, 1926.

Woolridge, Nancy Bullock. *The Negro Preacher in American Fiction before 1900*. Ph.D. diss. University of Chicago, 1942.

———. Review of *Say Amen, Brother!* by William H. Pipes. *Phylon* 12 (Fourth Quarter 1952): 396–97.

Wright, Richard. *12 Million Black Voices*. New York: Drummond, 1947.

———. *Lawd Today*. New York: Avon Books, 1963.

Yen, Alsace. "On Vladimir Propp and Albert B. Lord: Their Theoretical Differences." *Journal of American Folklore* 86 (April/June, 1973): 161–66.

Index

"spontaneous" composition, 46, 50, 59, 73
Strauss, David, 95, 96
structural units, of African-American sermon, 88; complicating segments, 91, 92, 110, 112; evaluation segment, 92, 93, 101, 110; orientation (introductory) segment, 91, 92, 110, 112; referential segment function, 90, 92, 112
Sutton-Smith, Brian, 36, 37
Szwed, John F., 103

Tales and Takings, 62
Taylor, Cecil, 96
theme, 25, 55, 60, 70, 74, 76, 106, 107; as both free-clause formula and bridge in key sermon, 59; defined, 45, 54; identifiable in key sermon, 56; as obligatory part of sermon structure, 55; "other worldly" character of African-American sermon themes, 62; synonymous with preacher's announced subject, 65
tradition, 30, 32; as ideas and basis of invention, 33
tradition bearers, active and passive, 27
Tubach, Frederich C., 83, 87

United Church of God in Christ, Inc., 6

verbal art (Bascom), 95
verbal mold, 19, 55, 56, 60, 61, 101; synonymous with performed African-American sermon, 65

Waletzky, Joshua, 88, 90, 92
Walker, Reverend Dr. Wyatt Tee, 41, 104
Watson, Reverend James, 43, 62
"weighted secular" factor (in African-American preaching), 19, 64, 104; in African-American sermon performance, 104; discussed, 60, 62
Welter, J. Thomas, 83, 87
"worrying" a line, 78, 96

Yoder, Don, 10
"You're Just Not Ready" (Cleveland), 1, 17, 35, 68, 70, 74, 81, 85, 88–89, 93, 97, 103, 104, 106; Cleveland's formulaic units, 59; formula, theme, and bridge readily identifiable in, 56; formula to theme relationship illustrated, 56–59; full text of sermon, 115–21; key sermon analysis, 17–24; preparatory modes, 17; preparatory modes illustrated, 18; sacred and secular factors in, 63